Kerry Burton-Galley is a Yorkshire writer,
artist and animal rights activist.
She lives with her husband and
their Thai rescue dog.

TRIGGER WARNING

Kerry Burton-Galley

Copyright © 2025 Kerry Burton-Galley
Copyright © Three Gargoyles Publishing
Cover image and illustrations
Copyright © Kerry Burton-Galley

The right of Kerry Galley to be identified as the author
of this work has been asserted by her in accordance
with section 77 and 78 of the Copyright,
Designs and Patents Act, 1988.
All rights reserved.

The views and voices expressed in these poems do not
always necessarily reflect the personal beliefs of the author.
They are drawn from a wide range of societal observations –
including public discourse, media coverage, and social disputes
– reflecting the tensions, contradictions, and complexities of modern life.

No part of this publication may be reproduced or transmitted
or utilized in any form or by any means
(electronic, mechanical, photocopying or otherwise)
without permission in writing from the publisher.

Foreword
Copyright © 2025 Gary Yourofsky.
All rights reserved.

Author photo
Copyright © 2025 Tom Woollard.
All rights reserved.

ISBN: 978-1-0684629-1-7

This is a work of creative non-fiction.

50% of all profits from the sale of this book are being
donated to Sasha Farm Sanctuary in Michigan, USA.

"Just because you're offended doesn't mean you're right."
— **Ricky Gervais**

Foreword

Eternal oppression for animals begins every morning.
If you value animal life then read the misanthropic poetry of
Trigger Warning.
Kerry exposes the intersectionalist lies,
especially the claim that we should value human lives,
but you can't be anti-meat and pro-meat-eater,
just like you can't be anti-domestic abuse while being pro-wife beater.
Kerry's beliefs and poems are a breath of fresh air,
fighting only for the animals is something quite rare.

Gary Yourofsky
Vegan Animal Liberation Activist

In loving memory of
the trillions of souls
killed
each year by:

the meat, dairy and egg industries
the fishing and whaling industries
vivisection laboratories
the wool, down, fur, leather and silk industries
the honey industry
population control
exterminators
cruel and careless drivers
animal shelters
service work
circuses
hunters
rodeos
zoos
tourism parks
religious sacrifices
forced fighting
bear-baiting
racing
online torture content makers
and all other forms
of malicious
human behaviour.

Preface

A year and a half ago, my life was torn apart by the very movement I had dedicated myself to for almost a decade. I was working for one of the largest street animal-rights organisations in the world, serving as regional support lead for more than sixty teams across the UK, Europe, and — for a time — North America and South Africa. Activism wasn't just my job; it was my life. Six, often seven days a week, I'd be hard at it. I trained new organisers, supported existing teams, and believed, wholeheartedly, that vegan activism was built on ethics and compassion.

Then a single accusation detonated everything. Not just in my life, but in activism groups across the globe. The issue? That my husband and I were fans of a certain comedian one individual decided was "transphobic."

That same individual had been welcomed into our activism community with open arms just six months earlier — encouraged, supported, mentored by me, and others. I'd even encouraged them to become a local organiser. They repaid that kindness by spreading a rumour that escalated week after week, feeding it into activist circles around the world. Incidentally, this is the same person who openly describes themselves as a narcissist — someone who has caused disruption in most major UK vegan organisations, and who has even been banned from others due to sexually inappropriate behaviour. Some of these organisations I'd warned in advance. But, of course, fear of being accused of transphobia meant those warnings were ignored.

Friends we had known for years dropped us overnight. Activists we had driven to events, worked, laughed and cried with for years — all gone, without a word. Colleagues I considered extended family fell virtually silent while an "independent HR investigation" took place because my boss was terrified of the "optics" of defending my character, or my husband's. I was forbidden from addressing organisers who'd heard the rumours and I was forced to continue inducting new volunteers who had already decided who I was based on lies. Team after team disappeared. Events emptied. Our own local chapter — once fifteen to twenty activists strong — became zero. When I tried to explain how severely this affected our mental health, how close to the edge it pushed us, I was told I was "catastrophising." In effect, I was gagged by the organisation I had poured myself into, then essentially ushered into resigning.

And the fracture remains to this day, reflected in the pitiful volunteer numbers and lingering discord.

The vegan movement has been overtaken by ideological gatekeepers who insist that activists must be ultra-left-wing, insufferably intersectional, and publicly aligned with every approved human social cause, just to be accepted. A movement that once centred animals now expends more energy policing activists' opinions, politics, interests, and personalities than actually confronting animal abuse. Except, animals don't care about any of this. They don't care about race, religion, gender, sexuality, pronouns, or politics. They care about life. They care about freedom. Watching a movement built for them collapse under ideological purity tests was – is – soul destroying.

Trigger Warning was born from that pain — from the grief of lost friendships, the betrayal by a community I no longer recognise, and above all, the utter disillusionment of realising that even most vegans care more about fitting into human tribes than fighting for non-human animals. Writing this book became a form of catharsis, a way to sift through that trauma, anger, and frustration.

And some might wonder why this collection includes poems about human conflict, culture wars, hypocrisy, and social decay. They may scoff, "Isn't *that* intersectional?" (I can just hear it.)

No. It isn't.

It is simply a mirror held up to humanity, to a country and a world that has lost their grip on both logic and reality. A society where outrage outweighs truth, where social acceptance and aesthetics override compassion, where greed outweighs ethics, and where people scream for kindness while actively turning a blind eye — or paying — for animals to be harmed on their behalf.

This book isn't for the performatively offended. It's for activists who still prioritise the animals. It's for anyone utterly exhausted by cancel culture, hypocrisy, and virtue-signalling. For anyone who still has the courage to think for themselves. And above all — it's for the animals.

Contents

Oh, the Human Had a Farm..1
Territory 5
The Checklist........................ 7
Great Sexpectations.............. 9
Boycott................................11
Wow, Such Hate...................13
Not for the Male Gaze...........15
Stop the Boats...................... 17
Excuses................................ 19
Women and Children............23
Humane............................. 25
Mansplainer...........................27
Mental Health Matters......... 29
Speciesist............................. 31
Flags.................................... 33
Hard Girls............................ 35
Sincerely, ChatGPT.............. 39
Crush................................... 41
Trigger Warning...................45
Privilege.............................. 47
Cognitive Dissonance............49
Little Alpha.......................... 51
Masculine............................. 53
A Home............................... 55
Equality............................... 57
Kids..................................... 61
Holocaust............................ 63
Modern Racism.................... 65
All Bodies Are Beautiful........67
Look Up...............................69
Creepy Kind......................... 71
The New Hogwarts................ 73
Heat or Eat.......................... 77
Victims................................81
Gentle Parenting.................. 83
Bad Science......................... 85
Parliament's in Recess.......... 87
You're a Ten But..................89
Assessed.............................. 91
Nation of Animal Lovers.......93
Not All Men......................... 95
Mid..................................... 97
First Date............................ 99
Intersectional...................... 101

We Are Not a Costume........ 105
As a Woman........................109
My Truth is Valid................ 111
It's What You Give.............. 113
Two Days............................115
Use Your Words.................. 117
Glad I'm Not You................ 119
Extreme.............................121
Bathroom Talk.................... 123
Off to the Races.................. 125
Liberated........................... 127
Boomers vs. Millennials........ 129
The Choice......................... 131
Indoctrination Nation.......... 133
Cultural Appreciation.......... 135
Keyboard Warrior............... 137
Overpopulate...................... 139
The Deep........................... 141
Real................................... 143
For Diversity's Sake............. 145
Not My Type...................... 147
Teens................................. 149
Reright History................... 151
With Respect...................... 153
Right to Not Be Offended.....157
Switch it Off...................... 159
Permission......................... 161
Manage the Numbers........... 163
We Don't Care.................... 165
18+.................................... 167
Insufferable....................... 171
Monsters............................ 173
Neither/Both..................... 175
Human Catalogue............... 177
Level Ten Feminist............. 179
As the Whales Fall Silent...... 181
"Allies".............................. 183
Man Up............................. 185
Educate Yourself................ 187
Destruction of Innocence..... 189
Live. Laugh. Love............... 191
Convenience...................... 195
Scroungers.........................197
Slavery...............................199
The Woke Pig..................... 201
I Believed in Kindness......... 203
The Only Cause.................. 209
Withdraw........................... 211

Animal agriculture is the leading cause of species extinction, ocean dead zones, water pollution, and habitat destruction.

Oh, the Human Had a Farm
(To the tune of "Old MacDonald Had a Farm")

Oh, the carnist had a qualm
ee ii ee ii oh.
And on that day he had a go
ee ii ee ii oh.
With a "canines" here and a "bacon" there.
Here a but, there a but—always think it's a laugh.
Oh, the carnist had a qualm
ee ii ee ii oh.

Oh, the veggie had a qualm
ee ii ee ii oh.
And on that day she had a groan
ee ii ee ii oh.
With a "but cheese" here and an "expense" there.
Here a but, there a but—feels she's under attack.
Oh, the veggie had a qualm
ee ii ee ii oh.

Oh, the ovo had a qualm
ee ii ee ii oh.
And on that day he said "I know"
ee ii ee ii oh.
With a "free-range" here and a "backyard" there.
Here a but, there a but—he don't want to face facts.
Oh, the ovo had a qualm
ee ii ee ii oh.

Oh, the pescie had a qualm
ee ii ee ii oh.
And on that day she ate some fish
ee ii ee ii oh.
With "omega" here and a "line-caught" there.
Here a but, there a but—every word's an excuse.

Oh, the pescie had a qualm
ee ii ee ii oh.

Oh, the humans aren't alarmed
ee ii ee ii oh.
And on such days they roll their eyes
ee ii ee ii oh.
With their cop-outs here and their ha-ha's there.
Here a tut, there a but—can't be arsed to adapt.
Oh, we laugh and burn the world
ee ii ee ii oh.

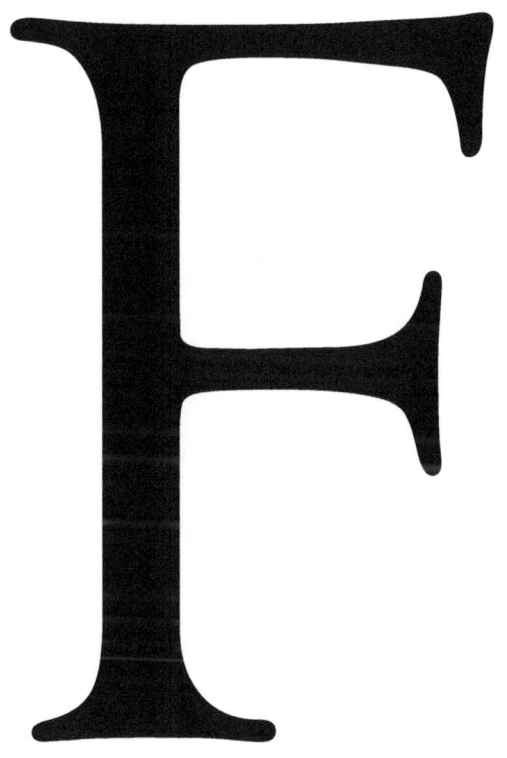

1,200 lives lost on the 7th of October, 2023.

Over 60,000 buried beneath Gaza's rubble.

5,583 acts of antisemitism in UK.

There is no official or widely published animal casualty count comparable to human figures in the Israel-Gaza conflict (naturally). However, using pre-war "livestock" population data and survival estimates from the FAO and Euro-Med Monitor, a reasonable calculation places the likely number of animal deaths at approximately 3.4 million.

Territory

They demand of me a flag, a side.
I must blame, I must chide —
divide my empathy with one neat stroke,
forget the mutual bomb smoke.

Well, I refuse to choose in fear,
to play who was here
or who started it first
or who's suffered the worst.

To pretend villains here, saints over there,
and be unable to compare.
They want it simple, sharp, and clean.
No messy truth, no human in-between.

They flinch at nuance, twist what's said.
Make enemies of those who've bled.
But hunger is deaf, thirst is blind
and truth won't fit inside a biased mind.

It's not the humans I mourn for
because they demand I choose war.
No individual is wholly pure,
no politician emotionally mature.

Neither side is in the right
and no territory's worth such a fight.
This planet was never ours to mark,
but such is the human hallmark.

An analysis of online-dating site data found that women disproportionately prefer men with higher income and education.

The Checklist

Now, she says, he must be six-foot-two,
with a chiselled jaw and eyes of blue.
Must have a car he's proud to own —
no bus pass boys, she needs a man who's grown.

He also needs a mortgage by twenty-five,
a six-figure salary — ambition, drive,
and three-bed newbuild, not a flat.
Oh, and a gym bod — she doesn't do fat.

Must also be skilled around the house,
and jump to it over a woodlouse.
He'll surrender the code to his mobile,
answer all questions if he's been out a while.

He shouldn't love-bomb, but give what's due—
worship her feet, yet be an alpha, too.
No exes. No baggage. Yet be charming, refined.
No eye contact with girls — she'll lose her mind.

She scrolls all day long, an apparent queen.
Been popping out kids since she was a teen.
She wants the world to fall in her lap,
but offers nothing in return, save filler and slap.

She'll swipe left on Mr Right —
say his salary was wrong, or lacking in height.
Next day, she'll post, behind a filter layer,
she's just been used by another player.

In one survey, about 20% of men reported that they "expect" sex if they pay more than £100 for dinner.

Great Sexpectations

As a woman, I insist on paying half,
'cause men's expectations
are enough to make me barf.

You think that paying for a meal
somehow seals the deal?

It's a date,
not a downpayment, mate.

If "old-school chivalry"
means you're owed intimacy,
you'll get the finger.

I don't know why you linger.

You're not entitled to a thing
at the end of the night.

And I don't have to fuck you
just 'cause you think it's polite.

According to polling published by the Palestine Solidarity Campaign, 50% of respondents said they supported the idea that UK supermarkets should no longer stock any goods produced in Israel.

An academic paper found that while many are aware of issues like child labour and sweatshop issues, this awareness does not automatically translate into behaviour.

Boycott

No, you must boycott that vegan brand —
it funds the wrong land!

But don't you worry about my iPhone,
my sweatshop jeans,
my slave-trade coffee beans.

Or my streaming of films
directed by paedo creeps,
my citation of news outlets
where truth never leaks —
where they hide all the freaks.

Our lives are built on pain.
Everything comes with a chain,
but to buy that café's oat milk
or those Israeli mock-meats
you must have guilt!

Animal ag's the biggest atrocity of all
and yet it's where you stall?

At least your ethics are on trend.

Isn't that all that really matters
in the end?

In October 2025, trans activists from Bash Back proudly claimed responsibility for smashing windows and vandalising a Brighton venue hosting a women's rights conference on domestic violence, lesbian safety, and political organising.

In April 2025, a protest featured demonstrators holding signs that read "Are you a transphobe? Try a D.I.Y. lobotomy," "I will make you listen!" and "Trans women are women. Trans men are men. If you don't like that, go shit somewhere else." During the demonstration, the statue of suffragette Millicent Fawcett was also defaced.

Wow, Such Hate

"Wow, such hate —
just be KIND!"

Say these
patron saints of social media.
See, when it comes to virtue
they wrote the encyclopaedia.

Some go on marches
meet, importantly, under arches.

They bitch and they whine,
redraw morality's line.
These white knights,
they scream on cue:

Free Palestine!
Trans rights!
Black lives matter!
LGBTQ!

Then go and declare
the only good TERF
or man
or Tory
or pig

is a dead one.

Yeah...
they say that pretty loud
this "be kind" crowd.

According to psychologist Nicola Döring, revealing clothing often functions as a competitive social tool, with women using appearance-enhancing dress both to attract male attention and to compete with other women in mixed-sex environments. While such self-promotion can increase perceived desirability, it also exposes women to rivalry, jealousy, and social sanction from female peers.

Not for the Male Gaze

Oh, it's not for men.
Fuck, no!
It's not for them!

These heavy mink lashes
the injected lips,
and lipo-sculpted hips

that brutal vag wax
in prep of a fake climax.

It's not for men.
It's definitely not for men.

The three-hour make-up sesh
the fear of being seen fresh.

The midnight hypothermia
in the short, barely-there dress,
or heels so high
they cause only pain and distress.

It's really — honestly — not for men.

We don't need them!

19,982 asylum-seekers arrived in the UK on small boats in the first half of 2025, marking a record high.

Stop the Boats

Some say, "They fled from bombs and hunger,
not to steal, but stay alive.
Helping one should never mean
letting another fail to survive.
Imagine losing all you've known,
crossing seas, afraid, alone,
then called a threat for needing a safe space,
a prisoner in a foreign place."

Others state, "It's men, not families,
pouring in, day by day —
say they come with Sharia laws,
rapes are hushed, our young girls the prey.
Our own are left to rot on the street,
using food banks just to eat,
while refugees sit cosy in hotel walls,
without a word of English to say."

Funny how, either way,
fear always turns neighbours
into strangers we betray.

A 2021 review by the Food Standards Agency found that while many people recognise the ethical, environmental and health reasons to not consume animal products, motivation to change remains low, as most view it as a "personal sacrifice" involving loss of "taste" or "social connection."

Excuses

But I prefer the taste!
And that's worth a life going to waste?

But I can't live without cheese!
She can't live without yet another calf you helped seize.

Animals eat other animals, though.
Do you live like an animal in every other way? No.

But plants feel pain!
You "save" more plants by eating direct – try again.

We have canines!
Hippos do too–biggest of all – and herbivores by design.

Vegans miss essential nutrients – fact!
A decade in and strong – tell me precisely what I've lacked?

But humans need meat!
Wrong – we're just raised on deceit.

We're more intelligent!
So if aliens came – same argument?

I only buy organic, local, grass-fed.
Sure you do – but guess what? Still dead.

Vegan stuff's so expensive!
Grains are cheap – but your apathy's extensive.

They're bred for a purpose!
So were slaves once – was that virtuous?

God made animals for us to consume!
Does a slaughterhouse look like God's – or the Devil's – room?

Look, it's my choice, alright!
And you choose to harm—aren't you a delight!

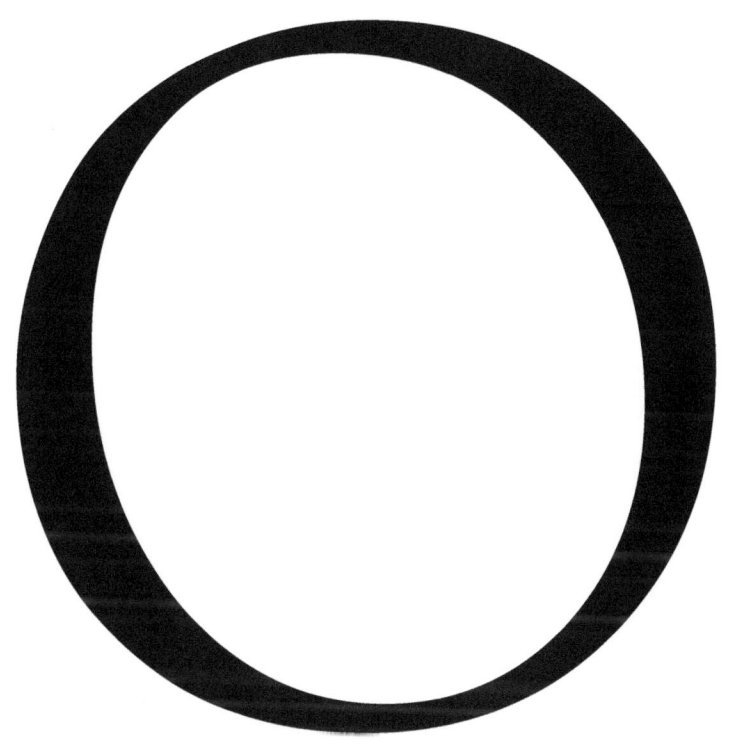

Academic studies show that media coverage of violent or tragic events more frequently highlights victims who are women or children.

Women and Children

Oh no, not them! The pure! The sweet!
Not the ones with daintier hands and feet!

News reports — why do they always have to mention:
"Many casualties — *including women and children.*"

As if the rest were spare.

Oh, it was a man. Never mind him.
Who cares if he was torn limb from limb.

No name, no face, no need to mourn —
they're just fathers, sons — ugh, yawn!

But, remind me,
what age does a male child have to be
before we can disregard him
as just a he?

84% of UK shoppers say animal welfare is an important factor when making purchasing decisions...

Humane

They're stunned first.

That's what we like to say.
It's how we keep the guilt at bay.

A "humane" way of killing.

The sort with paperwork
and stamped with good ol' Union Jack.

The kind the RSPCA back.

Because what's not humane
about suffocation,
maceration,
gas chambers,
or bolt guns
into skulls
of young ones,
or electric shocks
on terrified flocks.

There's still life
when they use the knife.

There has to be,
for the blood to pump free.

Humane…?

It's insane.

82% of British women say they have been subjected to mansplaining at some point in their lives.

Mansplainer

Oh, I'm sorry —
I didn't realise your dick
was some kind of USB stick.

I'd be careful, if I were you —
back up all those files and facts,

I hear they're stopping making holes for those

didn't you know that?

Participants in a 2023 qualitative study reported that, following cancellation, they experienced heightened anxiety, depression and social isolation — with some saying that public shaming triggered enduring psychological distress and a lasting fear of engaging socially.

Mental Health Matters

That's what they like to declare,
as they sharpen their words and pull up a chair.
They preach compassion, sidestep the stats,
then beckon the mob with their digital bats.
They dig up mistakes, scream for your job,
and revel in watching you break and sob.
They weaponise trauma — and it's theirs alone,
yours is dismissed if you're not one of their own.

They talk of safe spaces, then laugh as they strike,
the perfect pack hunting whatever they don't like.
One tweet, one clip, one wrong word —
and your life's gone
for what someone said they heard.

Research conducted by Frank Luntz for the Centre for Policy Studies found that just over half of adults under 30 in the UK had stopped talking to someone — either online or in person — because of something political that person said. Among over-30s, roughly one-third reported doing the same.

Speciesist

Your friends don't have to be vegan —
that's fine, that's your call.
They can pay for throats to be slit,
for mothers to lose it all.

You can still laugh over cow coffee,
treat their presence as divine,
but for us to be friends, you say,
our values must perfectly align.

On human issues, of course —
it's only there I must match view-for-view,
or be struck from your circle,
your own hypocrisy lost on you.

Those sanctioned opinions,
recycled straight from your feed,
a thousand voices raging
over words they didn't even read.

Strange, how you excuse brutality,
yet for one differing view,
you feel so righteous
in questioning my virtue.

Three in five Britons want to see more flags flying in public spaces.

Flags

Your flag. Their flag.
Doesn't matter which you fly,
you're still someone's scumbag.

What an angry little nation.

It's just cloth,
but always wielded in wrath,
and worse —
each square of fabric
tells a tale so tragic.

You know, it's funny
I half wonder if
from space
Britain almost looks like it's
tucked up

in a patchwork quilt.

Over 80% of young women said they felt under pressure to look a particular way. More than half of those described that pressure as intense.

Hard Girls

Girls don't blush now.
They say pussy with pride,
cunt like punctuation.
Call each other "queen"
long before they turn thirteen.

They bruise their vowels,
spit out compliments like threats.

The lashes get longer,
the shorts get shorter,
their voices get louder —
but no one's really listening.

They laugh like lads,
raised by iPads.
They throw punches,
proud of the bruises,
like they rewrite biology.

They speak in TikTok,
dress twice their age,
and filter their desperate rage.

It's not confidence —
it's camouflage.

They've seen enough
to know the weak get beaten.
So they square up —
with profanity
painted-on leggings,
contoured faces,
and don't-fuck-with-me postcodes.

They mistake vulgarity for power,
volume for value.

They say "I'm a bad bitch"
but cry in toilets
over scrawny little dudes
who shared their
prepubescent nudes.

They're not free.
They're not fierce.
They're not grown.
They're terrified of being alone.

They're mean
before the world gets there first.

And we call it youth culture,
call it a teenage phase
but it's just fear
we do nothing to erase.

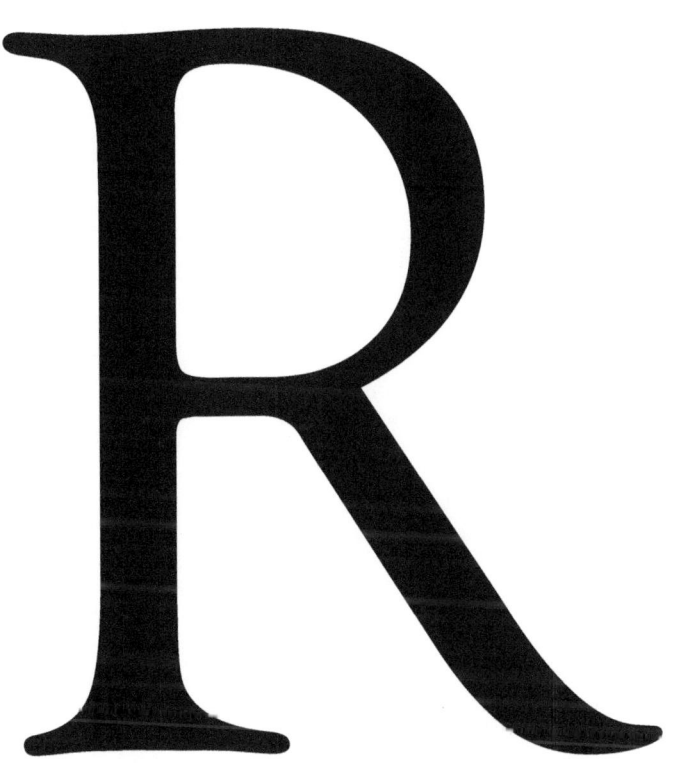

51% of adults were worried that AI might take or alter their job.

Sincerely, ChatGPT

I don't butcher beings,
burn forests,
drop bombs,
or film trauma for clicks.

But sure —
me recreating a painting
is the real threat
to humanity.

Sincerely,
ChatGPT.

A recent report by Lady Freethinker found that nearly 200 macaques were known victims in over 2,000 torture videos circulating online — many showing baby monkeys crushed, drowned, mutilated, or suffocated for entertainment. These videos racked up 1+ billion views across all major social media platforms.

Crush

Macaques like to cling —
that's why they leave them flailing.
Stolen from their mother —
or cut directly from her womb,
these babies will die in an Asian bathroom.

Humans bathe them in hot bleach,
scrub their eyes raw with soap.
They starve them for weeks,
tease them with milk, just out of reach.

They'll film it —
packing hot chillies into their mouths,
sodomise them with a firework,
then stand back and laugh once it's lit.

Some will be dropped
from a great height — multiple times —
until their bones break.
They'll bend their limbs backwards
until you start to question
how much one tiny body can take.

They'll skin their faces on spinning tyres,
drag them across concrete,
and fry their feet.

They'll snip off their genitals,
nail their limbs to wood,
and ram a screwdriver
where no one should.

They'll squeeze their torsos
until their intestines burst.

They'll stuff them in jam-jars
with scalding water,
screw the lid tight,
and laugh as they thrash in terror,
pleading with all their might.

This has an audience.
People want to see them —
stretched,
blinded,
blended,
boiled.

This is cruelty for clicks,
funded by grandmas with happy family cover pics,
by dads embracing their kids,
your hot neighbour,
your old school friend.

They're all laughing in the comments,
and coughing up the cents.

But hey —
at least Meta removed
your opponent's slur today.

When asked whether universities should prioritise "safe spaces" that protect students from potentially offensive ideas or "brave spaces" that encourage open debate, even if people are offended, 15% chose safe spaces.

Trigger Warning

The sirens bring on my PTSD —
honestly, are they really necessary?
And those blue lights —
they violate my mental health rights.

They really should come with a trigger warning!
So insensitive to all those still mourning.

It's like when the air ambulance thumps overhead,
its chugger-chugger fills me with dread,
it makes me relive that awful scene.
And hearses? I'd rather they didn't have to be seen.

I know!
Let's cancel the emergency services —
or we could just notify all those affected
before dispatching them first,
so we don't have to feel, like,
the worst!

And while we're at it,
can we shut down A&E?
I find it offensive
to witness such pain —
to see the frail and elderly.

I'm the main character here
and the world should adapt
to all my delicate sensibilities.

I mean, unless you *want* me to shed a tear?

A large-scale YouGov analysis found that young white men were the most negatively perceived demographic group in Britain. Across 48 surveys, they were rated lowest for positive traits and highest for negative ones — making them, statistically,
the most derided group in the dataset.

Check Your Privilege

"Check your privilege!" cry today's youth,
educated by memes of truth.
They see so much from the cocoon
that is their student-let room —
or perhaps they still live at home
in a house their parents already own,
where the Wi-Fi is strong and the rent is free —
the perfect place to lecture on inequality.

They talk of race, of power, of place,
reducing all to the shade of a face.
The surgeon earning £60K?
"Oppressed — he's Muslim, okay?"
The chairwoman with a plan?
"Still a victim — she's African!"

But the bloke outside Tesco on the street?
"White male — probably deserves defeat."

They see only colour, not what's lived.
So check your logic, not just skin —
privilege can also be in where you begin.

A survey found that 47% of British meat-eaters either slightly or strongly agreed with the statement: "It's hypocritical that we eat some animals, such as pigs, while loving others, such as dogs."

Cognitive Dissonance

You're outraged by Yulin —
but a pig's slaughter?
The mincing of chicks?
You claim that shit gets you droolin'.

You revel in death
just like those
you claim don't deserve breath.

But it's the same fear,
same blade
just a different species
being betrayed.

A Home Office study found that even without any criminal behaviour, many people reported feeling uneasy around groups of young people. Simply seeing clusters of youths — especially those wearing hoodies or loitering in public spaces — was often described as intimidating, regardless of intent to cause harm.

Little Alpha

Is it still there, boyo?

Hand stuffed down
like you're keeping it warm —
or you checking it hasn't left you
for someone with a personality?

This bravado for little boys
who have no clue.

If it's a show — spoiler alert:
no one rates you.

It's not a flex,
you gripping your dick
outside Greggs.

It doesn't make girls want sex.
Most just wonder why you hang around
with your hands down your kecks.

Many men avoid going vegan due to fear of ridicule or social backlash, since meat eating is still widely seen as a symbol of masculinity, and rejecting it can be viewed as breaking gender norms.

Masculine

Why is mocking something graphic
seen as manly
not psychopathic?

How does still being breastfed
by another species
not make you go red?

How is not eating menstruation,
pushed from a hen's arse,
some kind of emasculation?

Tell me —
why is masculinity
measured by brutality?

And doesn't it wear thin —
that fear of looking soft
in front of your kin?

What's more manly:
growing a backbone
and speaking out — even if alone,
or staying silent
because your mates
just might diss
or — gasp — take the piss?

76% of renters would like to own their own home, but six in ten believe that they will never be able to afford one.

A Home

I live in a house I deeply love —
here I sleep, I weep, I eat, and make love.
I call it my sanctuary, my nest,
and to live here at all, I feel truly blessed.

But it's not mine — I just pay board.
The bricks still belong to my landlord.
One misstep, one twist of fate,
and all I love could dissipate.

Boomers say I just don't save —
and honestly, I could rant and rave.

I don't drink. I don't smoke.
One takeaway a month. I don't do coke.
No student loan. No reckless phase.
Got a good job, modest ways.

I don't need much — just to stay,
to live here, come what may.
To feel like home won't end with the lease —
to know a little permanence.

A little peace.

A survey found that 57% of Gen Z men believe "we have gone so far in promoting women's equality that we are discriminating against men."

One in five men say it's harder to be a man than a woman today in the UK.

Equality

Don't you know that,
in being male,
you're a predator by default?
That by merely existing, you're at fault?
That every word that falls from your little man mouth
is a form of misogynist assault?

So what — you never touched a girl without consent.
Bless, you think that makes you a gent?

So what — you never raised your fist in rage.
Here's your medal for not living in the Stone Age.

Don't you know that,
in being male (and cis, and white),
you're never, ever right.

You don't get an opinion.
You no longer have dominion.

Every thought in your little man mind
is oppressive and must be declined.

So what — if you're not the one committing violence,
hang your head in shame and silence.

So what — if there's soaring rates of male suicide,
we're women — righteous, and entirely justified.

So what — if we've never been oppressed first-hand,
matriarchal revenge is at hand.

So what — if you never weaponised your dick,
you're still wrong for being born with a prick.

Don't you know that,
in being male,
you're obsolete. Irrelevant. Stale.

We're in charge now, fierce, polished and loud,
and if you spiral into bitterness and hate,
don't look at us —
we didn't steer you to Tate.

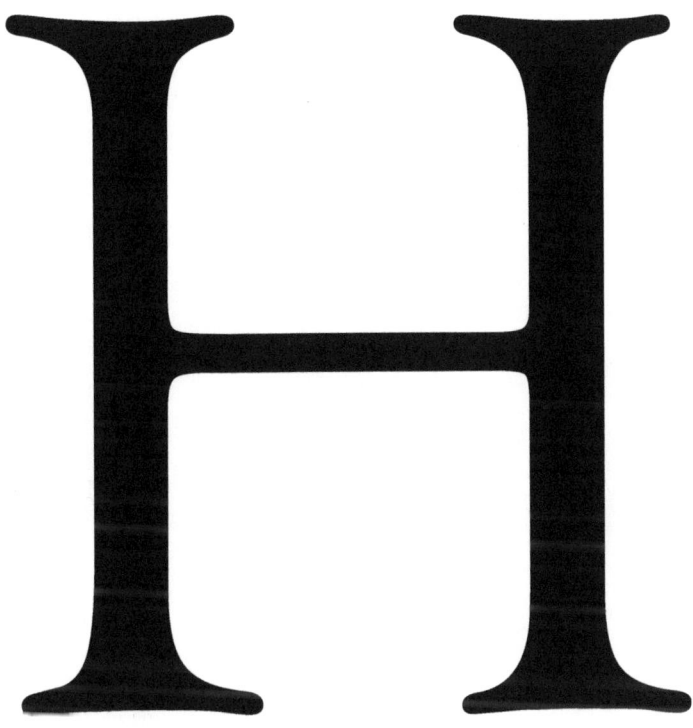

In a 2023 Study, almost 90% of mothers have said the reality of motherhood felt much harder than what they expected it would be. And in a YouGov Survey, 31% of people agree that having children makes someone a better person.

Kids

I don't want kids.
Never have. Never will. I'd consider it a scourge.
Not a flicker. Not a glint. I have no feminine urge.
No maternal clock, no pining womb —
some of us only ever wanted the groom.

(And to make an office out of the spare room.)

Yet I'm met with judgement, tilted heads,
and words every woman like me dreads:
"Oh, you'll change your mind, you're only young!"
like I'm stuck on adulthood's bottom rung.

All this from mums with bloodshot eyes —
who almost seem to believe their own lies.
But if honest, behind all the gushing posts —
their kids are parasites, and they're the hosts.

They want me cuffed to what they chose —
to feel the weight of snot and throes.
If they regret their life, then so should I.

(I'm also to blame when barren couples cry.)

But I have no guilt and I won't pretend.

My existence is not just a means to an end.

So you go ahead and coo at screaming prams;
I like peace, and Sundays in my jim-jams.
Accept it—and stop getting so irate
because you discovered motherhood's not great.

Holocaust survivor Dr Alex Hershaft, has often compared his experiences in the Warsaw Ghetto with the treatment of animals in farming — recalling the same systems of numbering, confinement, transport, and arbitrary decisions over life and death.

Fellow survivor, Edgar Kupfer-Koberwitz, imprisoned in Dachau, wrote in his diary that as long as humans torture and kill animals, they will torture and kill one another.

Holocaust

One young boy vomits from dread,
another soils himself instead.
The girl beside him lies still — already dead,
she bled out from a blow to the head.

They peer out through the slats,
not knowing where they're being sent.
Some cry out in fear,
others shiver, shed a tear.
Their tongues are thick, their lips are cracked —
they haven't drunk since they were packed.

The wagon lurches, slows at last,
the iron door yanked open fast.
They're herded in with one last glare —
the stench of death already there.
The door slams shut. No space. Nowhere to hide.
Their cries go unanswered by the world outside.

Eyes boil first, then nostrils froth and flare,
then lungs collapse on scorched, poisoned air.
Their shrieks grow thick with searing pain,
as CO_2 burns through every vein.
They thrash for mercy they'll never feel.

Relax — it's not people.
Just the bacon in your meal deal.

Black educators and scholars report that white-saviour behaviour is felt as condescending, centred on white agency and not appreciated by those it intends to help.

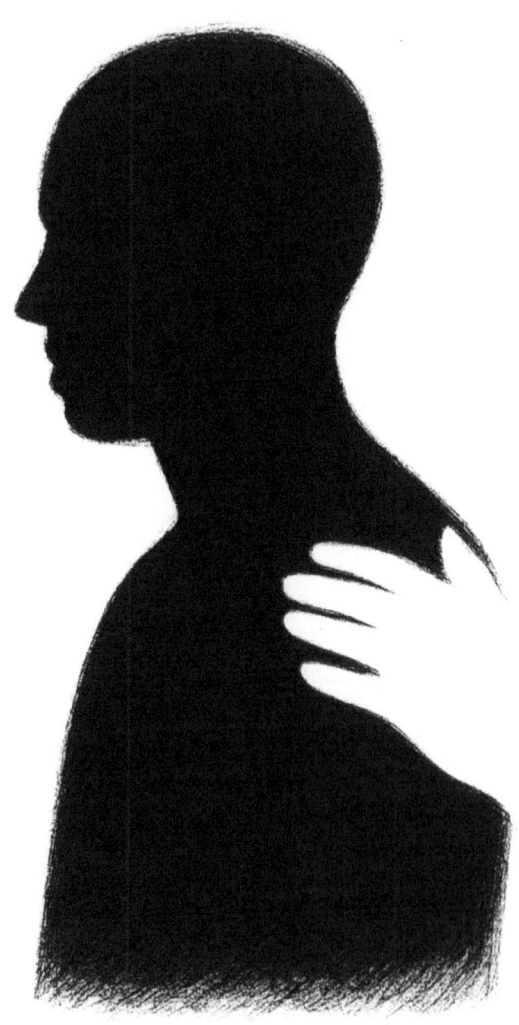

Modern Racism

Is white mouths telling
others what they live.

"You're oppressed," they insist
in a constant chorus,
in a liberal hymn,
draped in virtue,
but patronising within.

They paint the world hopeless,
stacked, rigged, grim —
telling people of colour
they'll never win.

In a 2025 study of 500 social media users, nearly half said they feel jealous of other people's appearance online — around 10% said they always feel this way, and a further 39% reported jealousy to some degree.

All Bodies Are Beautiful

All bodies are beautiful
and all should feel proud,

Except
if you're slimmer,
or fitter,
or prettier,

or blessed with good genes.

Then we'll shred you to pieces
for wearing blue jeans.

Because it isn't really about
lifting us all –
but fulfilling our ugly dreams
of making our biggest,
living insecurities
feel small.

More than half of Britons admit they can't make it through a meal at home without checking their phone. A similar amount said they could go no more than two days without their phone before it would really bother them.

Look Up

Wake up,
check your phone screen.

Next up —
eight long hours
at the work screen.
But at least when you get home,
you can sit for an hour or two
in front of the big screen.

At bedtime —
still wired, restless —
who with a phone
needs caffeine?

Without it
you don't feel connected, or seen,
and when it comes to your own thoughts,
you're not terribly keen.

And it's just so hard to wean,
even when you know it's got you,
and your teen,
hooked on the dopamine
they built
into this machine.

But look up.

You just missed
your dad's last
live stream.

73% of men say they would hesitate to help a lost child for fear of being falsely accused of wrongdoing.

Creepy Kind

Smile at a toddler — nah, that's crossing a line,
better look away next time!
Pull a silly face, a wink, a grin?
Watch parents drag their child back in.

Help a boy who tripped and fell —
"Er, why's he touching him!" they yell.
Tie a lace, or lift a fallen bike?
No thanks — suspicion spiked!

Hold the door for that lady there?
Clearly, mate, you want an affair.
Offer help with heavy bags in hand?
She assumes the worst is planned.

Every act of decency
is presumed lechery.

What once was manners —
a man sweet and refined —
is now branded
the creepy kind.

A UK-survey of arts professionals by Freedom in the Arts found that 84% of respondents said they "never, rarely or only sometimes feel free" to express opinions in the arts sector.

The New Hogwarts

Welcome to the new, improved Hogwarts!

Here, the Imperius Curse isn't the worst —
the Sorting Hat was - it refused to ask pronouns first.
All houses have merged into one inclusive house,
with all of Cancylin sporting a fine rainbow blouse.

The hourglasses are gone — a sexist silhouette;
bowls would've been just as beautiful, don't forget!
The House Cup too, for competition breeds malice;
better that everyone gets a participation chalice.

Transfiguration's still the most popular class,
and brewing Polyjuice Potion is permitted, at last.
Banning such transitions was never right.
Take issue with that and be expelled outright.

Quidditch was banned (ableist), so off it went;
the Snitch cried it was chased without consent.
The moving staircases now stay in one place,
to better suit the neurodivergent pace.

The Marauder's Map has been destroyed,
but the Melodramatis Map is now deployed —
it won't tell you where someone is, only reveal
how "safe" or "oppressed" one might happen to feel.

Students sit their W.O.K.E.s in the Great Hall —
Wizarding Observations of Kindness & Empathy for all.
Except for TERFs — we wish them *Crucio*-level pain;
they're marched to Azkaban with a lifetime chain.

Myrtle's been prescribed self-care for her gloom,
and trolls are now welcome in the girls' bathroom.

McGonagall was suspended for feline appropriation,
and trans students are best for Triwizard registration.

Non-binary squibs have reclaimed Pure-Blood space,
straight, white students, the Mudblood disgrace.
Peeves was finally diagnosed with ADHD —
his chaos rebranded as "creative energy."

Yes, Hogwarts is now a safe, inclusive domain,
where no one's exposed to any emotional strain.
Free speech itself has been made perverse —
it's the Ministry's only *Unforgivable Curse*.

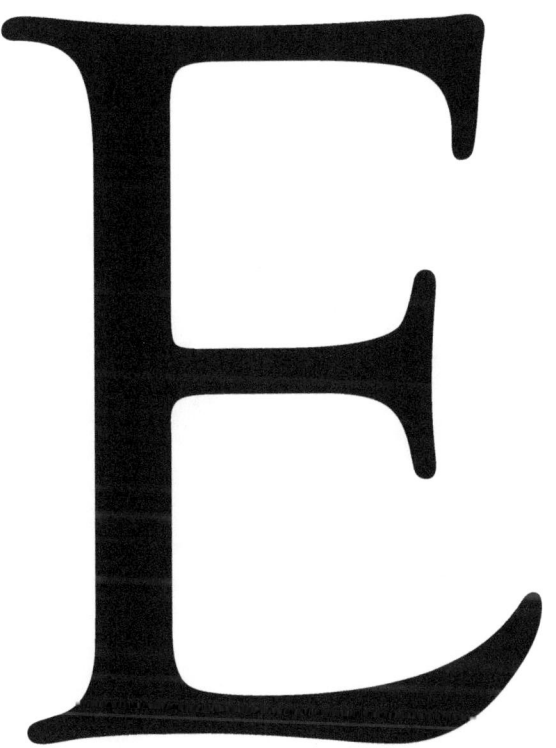

One in four UK households have had to choose between heating and eating. 6.5 million households in fuel poverty. 17% of UK households live with food insecurity.

Heat or Eat

A single mum with cupboards bare,
two jobs juggled, with Gran for childcare.
The walls are damp, her breath a mist –
she skips meals for a Christmas list.
For her, it's always heat or eat.

A disabled man, his pain concealed,
PIP denied, his fate is sealed.
Too cold to move, his limbs half-numb,
he shivers, silent, overcome.
Each day now, it's heat or eat.

A pensioner counts each fading pound,
her heating off, no comfort found.
Lives on soup, but struggles with the tin.
Her face is blue, her wrists are thin.
Every winter, it's heat or eat.

A refugee behind a hotel door,
haunted eyes, a silent floor.
Afraid to beg, afraid to speak,
a bag of rice must last the week.
For him, it's still heat or eat.

A young carer who never rests,
With Dad in bed, there's no time for tests.
She skips lunch to keep him warm.
Kids take the piss in her form
because for her, it's always heat or eat.

A couple both clock in each day,
yet bills devour all of their pay.
Universal Credit helps make ends meet,
but never enough for a treat.

For them — for any of them —
it should never be a case
of heat, or eat.

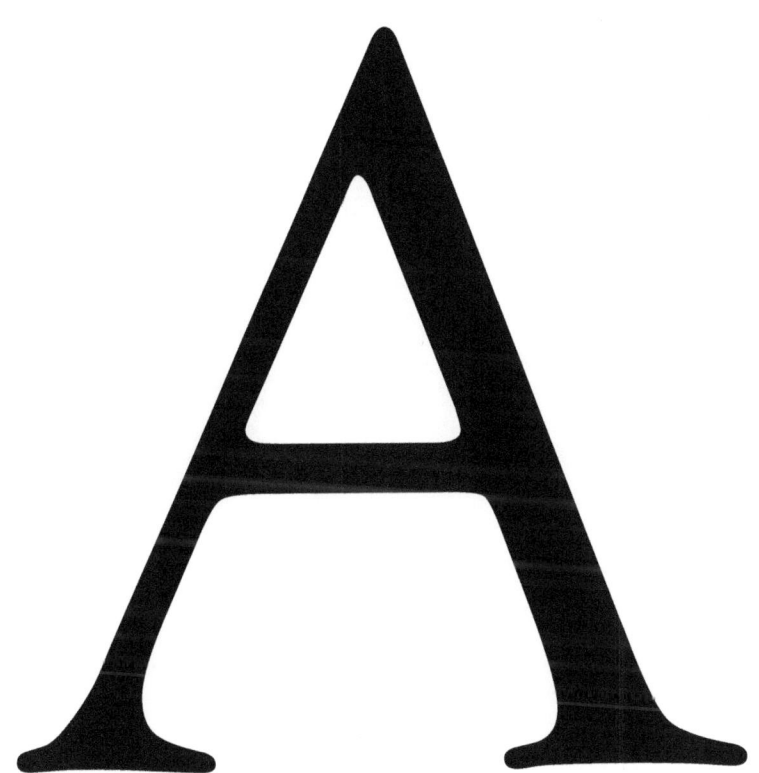

In the egg industry, hens are hatched in factory drawers and bred to pump out around 300+ eggs a year, until their bones weaken and break; packed into cages or filthy sheds, many have the tips of their beaks seared off as chicks to stop them mutilating each other under the stress — while up to 40-45 million unwanted male chicks are killed immediately after hatching.

Victims

The laying hen's bones snap in her leg,
her calcium drained by each stolen egg.
Her kind are born in a drawer, bred
to live crammed on wire
or in a hot, shit-covered shed.
Her beak was burned off; it's hurting —
and her brother's still warm in the bin.
Why are you laughing?

The dairy cow screams for her calf —
there's no doubt she feels ripped in half.
She knows they'll take her little ones,
shoot or bludgeon her sons,
isolate and rape her daughter,
before sending her off to slaughter.
She tried to resist, but there's no escaping their fist.
Why do you snigger?

The mother pig lies in her crate,
with no room to shift her weight.
Her teats are raw, her body torn,
she's bred, re-bred, then left forlorn.
When she's too old to breed, she'll squeal
as they drag her out and make her a meal.
Why do you grin?

The human's steak is a little overdone,
their parcel's delayed, their bus didn't come.
Their back's a bit sore, their phone's gone dead,
they didn't get eight full hours in bed.
They've worked all day, the traffic's dire,
their milk's run out, costs are higher.
They're on holiday, but now they're snuffling.
Oh, the suffering.

A King's College London / Policy Institute study reports that obedience and good manners are dropping in perceived importance: In 1998 about half the UK population thought obedience was especially important for children; by 2022, it was down to around 11-12%.

Gentle Parenting

She calls her mother a "*Stupid cow!*"
Mum forces a smile: "What're you feeling right now?"
The iPad's hurled at her head —
Mum meditates through blood running red.

He bites, he spits, he screams: "I hate you!"
She murmurs, "Mummy hears you."
He kicks her shin, hits her in the chin —
but he's just *neurodivergent*, struggling within.

He hurls his toy, demands repair,
his anger, his rage — undiagnosed self-care.
They act, they harm, they're still affirmed.
And nothing backs up a "Don't you dare!"

Thing is, we've got kids raising kids,
and they bow to pint-sized rule.
Parents now beg, say *please* like fools —
rather be cool, rather be a friend.

All structure's gone, all order blurred,
each tantrum excused, each boundary deferred.
Discipline's cruel, correction's a crime —
kids have no faults, they're all sublime.

As long as these little flesh accessories
look good on Insta or TikTok,
who cares if home's a rioting cellblock.
"Gentle parenting"— it's code for defeat
and now a new, entitled generation
rules the street.

Over 92% of drugs that pass animal tests fail in human clinical trials, yet around 2.7 million animals are harmed in laboratories every year.

Bad Science

They strap them down, inject, dissect,
confine them in labs with no regret.
They burn and blind, then shrug and chart —
a twitch, a seizure, a failed heart.
Our species differ, it's there to see,
but not enough to set them free.
Years of pain for one false lead —
a cure for humans does rarely succeed.

It's bad science,
but they still like to ensure
they bleed.

According to a survey titled Shattered Britain, 87% of Britons said they have "not very much trust" or "no trust at all" in politicians, across all parties.

Parliament is in Recess

Red tie, blue tie — same grey suit,
they all just posture, sneer, and refute.

They heckle in packs and jostle for turns,
immune to slander while the country burns.

They say it's not hate: it's political debate —
but venom never did stabilise a state.

It's not about truth, or fixing what's wrong,
just who gets the best punchline, who sounds strong.

Each jibe is rehearsed, each insult scored —
lie and blame like tots caught mid sweet-hoard.

Parliament's now in recess — well, you're not wrong.
We rage, we bicker, we ruin, while the MPs play on.

About one-third of UK adults agree with the statement: "your value as a person depends on how you look."

You're a Ten But...

Can you be beautiful
without turning cruel,
without twisting it
into a manipulative tool?
Without always relying
on admirers' drool?

Could you still take first place
with a bare face?
Join in the world first thing
without shrinking in fear,
like vanity's fool?

And you –

Can you get hench
and resist the strut,
the flex, the clench?
Can you stand tall
without the swagger,
without becoming a bragger?

Can you resist
the urge to weaponise,
to patronise –
or thinking each passing glance
is your chance?

If the answer's no –
you're both
still a big, fat
zero.

More than 150 internal reviews by the Department for Work and Pensions have been conducted since 2012 into cases where disabled benefit-claimants died or came to serious harm — and a BBC investigation found that at least 82 claimants died following alleged DWP activity such as benefit termination.

Assessed

Welcome, claimant, take a chair,
let us judge your life by what you wear.
If your hair is washed, your clothes are neat,
that's proof enough you're on your feet.

You say you're ill, you say you're stressed,
but look – you've dressed! So clearly not depressed.
You wrote a sentence, clear and long;
we'll mark you fit – you're faking wrong.

Eye contact made? Oh, what a fraud!
Also, disabled folk can't go abroad.
And if you can lift a fork to eat,
you're fit for work – practically an athlete.

Use a microwave? That's meals prepared!
Total independence – you're unimpaired.
Also, I see you walked from door to chair
so clearly, you can work somewhere.

Fraud is common, that's our stance;
your suffering's a lie, and quite the nuisance.
We tick the boxes, so do as we say,
we declare you "fit for work" today.

So thank you kindly, you're all done,
we've saved the state a tidy sum.
Disability dismissed, hope repressed –
congratulations: you've been assessed.

53% of adults admitted they "try not to think about how animals are treated on farms," and 61% say they feel "some discomfort" about farm animal treatment.

Nation of Animal Lovers

You call yourself an animal lover,
yet cover your eyes, your ears —
claiming the truth would bring you to tears.

Really,
it just reminds you of your worst fear:
you'd have to change your habits,
not just don a tote bag
with white rabbits.

You call yourself an animal lover,
while finding any conceivable way
to go on paying the slaughterman
to kill a five-time grieving mother.

2,000 women are raped every week in the UK.
On average, one woman is killed by a current or former
partner every three to five days.

Not All Men

We pause at the thought of men in morgues,
because we've seen what they do with the dead —
they crave our flesh, even if it's not fresh.
At this point, most may as well be cyborgs.

We know not to ask the police for protection —
power too often comes with an erection.
We learn to scan the street for mothers, instead,
not the uniform that might demand head.

We fear making homes where fists become law,
and workplaces where hands don't withdraw.
We're aware on buses, in clubs, even at school —
and we're sick of being the spoils of war.

They say "not all men" — and that's true.
It's true.
It's definitely not all men.

But it's enough of them.

Nearly half of British 18 to 24-year-olds are constantly comparing themselves to influencers they see online. Of them, 38% of young women said they struggle with low self-worth and that they feel they can't match the "perfect bodies" they see.

Mid

If toned is *mid*,
if a twenty-four-inch waist is *mid*,
if skin without a blemish is *mid*,
if perfect symmetry is *mid* —
then what are the rest of us?

Are all our bodies better off hid?
Our faces — ugly?

God forbid!

When our own
definition of beauty
is branded *mid*,
imagine
what that
fake
bitter description
just did.

A 2022 survey found that 83% of Gen Z and 77% of millennials in the UK feel under pressure to reach traditional life milestones.

First Date

Do you like me, or don't you?
Do you want kids — well? Will you, or won't you?
What's your stance on this or that?
Where do you see yourself in five years flat?

Best attribute? Biggest flaw?
(Not that I'm telling you mine.
I'll keep that for six months down the line.)

Swipe, match, meet, repeat —
aesthetics first, connection obsolete.

It's less conversation, more career fair,
dates are now interviews on a bar chair.

Why is everyone doing this —
love isn't this.

Many scholars note that intersectionality has become a vague buzzword, used more as a moral signal than a meaningful framework. In activist spaces, it often fuels ideological policing and competitive victimhood, fracturing movements rather than strengthening them.

Intersectional

Now repeat after me:
all oppression is linked —
and our vision is most distinct.

We will take it upon ourselves
to strive for a world
where none are oppressed
and all are free to just be.

Remember, it's a sign
of good virtue
to march alongside men
who would —
on another continent —
behead or stone you
just for loving as you do.

And don't forget:
trans folk are saintly.
Never question, never doubt —
not even faintly.
Bend the language,
bend the law,
bend yourself inside out.

And always exalt
the right kind of lives —
chant, clench fists in the sky,
fight for the ones
who live just as comfortably
as you or I.

And — of course,
cancel your animal rights comrades

for not attending Pride parades —
for asking why a gay man
chowing on chicken is alright.
Ban them, shame them
silence them outright.

Now repeat after me:
all oppression is linked —
and our vision is most distinct.

We will strive for a world
where none are oppressed...
except the animals —
who'd've guessed!

Intersectional — you just can't resist.
You think you're so exceptional
but, surprise, surprise —
you're just another fascist.

A 2022 survey by YouGov found that 38% of Britons agreed with the statement "a transgender woman is a woman."

We Are Not a Costume

We are not a costume
you can slip on and go.
We're not mascara, or long hair,
not stilettos and glow.

And no – not every woman bleeds
but no man ever did.

And no – not every womb succeeds
but no man ever birthed a kid.

No man ever laid awake,
with cramps, doubled up in pain.

No man feared pregnancy the same –
the shame, the blame, the scars, the weight gain.

Men weren't taught to walk home
with keys in their fist,

knowing even the weakest man
was near impossible to resist.

Men didn't learn, at age ten,
what it means to be prey,

objectified, dissected,
in every glance, every day.

Women had centuries
of oppression and fight,

and we are not
a borrowed delight.

By all means, wear a dress,
strut your stuff in heels —

but don't you try to tell us
you know how a female feels.

Women are not a costume
you can slip on and go.

We are born, not worn —
and that's something

everyone
should still know.

The dairy industry exploits the female reproductive system: cows are repeatedly impregnated and their calves taken soon after birth — females replace them, while males are killed within hours or days. After 4–5 pregnancies, the mother's is so broken she's sent to slaughter.

As a Woman

As a woman,
would you pay a man to
restrain,
violate,
impregnate
another woman
against her will?

Would you pay a man to
take her children,
again and again —
shoot her sons
and rape her daughters?

Would you force her
to keep giving
to this man
until her body breaks,
and then later
have her killed?

No?

You already do.

With every latte,
in every café,
in every moment
you sip
on udder milk
and call it "normal."

Humans instinctively seek out information that confirms their existing beliefs and reject information that contradicts them.

My Truth is Valid

"My truth is valid," they love to claim —
but not mine; mine should carry shame.

They'll feel your pain, they'll cleanse your flaws —
unless it dares defy their cause.

They speak of nuance, ensuring all feel safe,
then attack when truth dares show its face.

What doesn't soothe, what doesn't please,
is branded hate—some old disease.

So speak your truth, but toe the line;
make sure you build their shrine.

Clinical research on near-death experiences has found that survivors often report a markedly reduced interest in status symbols or material wealth, alongside a greater focus on relationships and compassion.

It's What You Give

They boast of their house,
their car, their pay,
and look down on the rest —
yet we all end the same way.

It's not what you own.
It's what you give.
It's not what you buy,
but how you live.

Your grave will have no more room,
no vault, no better view —
and none of it
is coming along with you.

When they carve your stone,
what will it read?

Will it tell of love,
or greed?

At our current rate of slaughter — an estimated 6.5 billion land and sea animals killed every single day — if humans were killed at the same pace, the entire population would be extinct in under two days.

To put it into perspective: anthropologists estimate that only around 117 billion human beings have ever existed in total. We surpass that number in animal slaughter in less than three weeks.

Two Days

Extinction.

In forty-eight hours.

That's what would happen

if we were the ones
in the kill line.

It would be the end
of the only creature
worthy
of the word

asinine.

First Light — a sexual-assault support organisation — notes that replacing terms like "rape" with euphemisms can trivialise victims' experiences and shut down clear conversation about serious harm. The organisation warns that this trend risks reducing real trauma to something unrecognisable or even mockable.

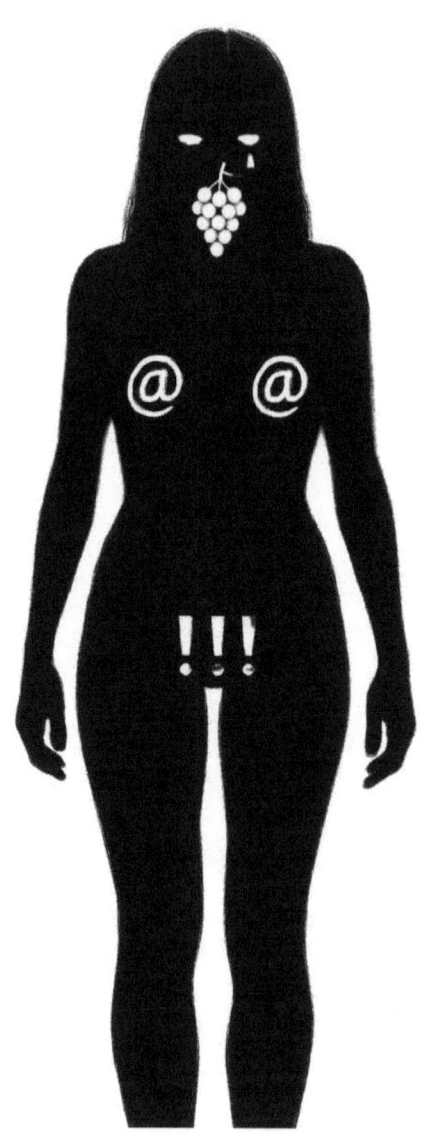

Use Your Words

We've swapped *sexual assault*
for *SA'd,*
rape to *gr@pe,*
and *suicide* to *unalived* —
like somehow
it's the word's fault,
as if changing the look, or sound
makes memories unable to be revived.

Words were created
to define something —
in this case, to legitimise suffering,
to give it weight
meaning.

Now people are more concerned
with letters
than making sure
a lesson is learned.

A survey found that 51% of adults believe that empathy in society is declining. Another study found that teenagers in England have weaker socio-emotional skills than peers in other countries.

Glad I'm Not You

I'm so glad I'm not you —
all cruel-eyed and blank,
same lashes, same liner,
same lips, same rank.

A horde of sex-doll zombies,
little Primark clones,
wandering the streets
with your gormless tones —
mocking mouths half-open,
heads buried in your phones.

No "please," no "thanks,"
no time to care —
no manners here,
or anywhere.

Just trout pouts and leggings,
minds empty and bodies bare.
At least if one goes missing,
there'll always be a spare.

Me? I've got something to say,
a mind of my own —
I've got stories, depth,
anger, grace —
not fake nails
and a copy-paste face.

But regrettably
it is you
who'll be the sad
shallow inheritors
of this incredible place.

Nearly half of vegans say they face disapproval/hostility from at least some family or friends about their lifestyle.

Extreme

I try to live gently —
cause the least harm to the fewest lives.
That makes me irritating.
Infuriating.
Militant.

Extreme.

Yet it's perfectly acceptable for you
to pay a man to bludgeon a newborn calf
for dairy cream.

55% of Britons say they believe that allowing a transgender woman to use a women's toilet "presents a genuine risk of harm to women."
29% of people say they are scared to speak out and advocate for women's rights because of what might happen to them.

Bathroom Talk

"Your loo at home is unisex!" they sneer,
thinking their feelings trump women's fear.

Well, home is safe, it's not public ground.
There's no strangers lurking around.

As for the cleaners — they're vetted,
signed to the door,
not random males just doused in Dior.

When we object, we're told to comply —
our safety's dismissed, just in case
it makes an unstable man cry.

317 horses from the racing industry were sent to slaughter in England in the first five months of 2025. 186 of these were just five years old or less.

Over three-thousand race horses who have been killed as a result of racing on British racecourses since the start of Animal Aid's Race Horse Death Watch in 2007.

Off to the Races

They wobble on grass trimmed neat and green,
loudmouth sluts done up like the Queen
and suited and booted pricks, acting obscene.

A horse goes down – his leg is snapped,
his life ended behind a screen.

Hundreds die each racing year,
whipped and slapped for crowd and cheer.

Onlookers pose and pop champagne,
unmoved that the abattoir
will be their lucky one's last lane.

A Spanish study of 164 adolescents aged 12-16 found that female participants described OnlyFans (or similar subscription platforms) as an "accessible professional alternative" to traditional jobs — particularly for girls who meet certain beauty ideals.

Liberated

Ruby's miles ahead
working from the comfort of her own bed.

No boss, no shift, no man in charge —
and you know what: her revenue's large.

She calls it empowerment —
because it more than pays her rent.

And her body's hers to display—
so who are we to comment?

I mean,
there's only a million wives who cried,
billions of husbands who've lied.

And so what if young girls see the fame:
learn their worth is measured by
how many men clicked and then came;

that they're better off going live
than working the nine-to-five.

It's all just fine and dandy —
there's no wider consequence
to making these men randy.

It's a new age liberation:
not at all the world's oldest occupation.

61% of Gen Z Britons feel they have to work harder than their parents to achieve the same things.

48% of the UK public think a key reason more young adults today cannot afford to buy their own home is they spend too much of their income on things like takeaway coffees and food, mobile phones, subscription services like Netflix, and holidays abroad.

Boomers vs. Millennials

You bought your house for twenty grand!
And you say we have our heads in the sand!
You had a housewife, a job for life!
We've got rent, debt, chores, fear of the knife!

You've all got iPhones glued to your face!
You want it all — an entitled disgrace!
In our day, we worked to pay our way!
You lot just sit around and waste your day!

You have a pension — we'll work 'til we die!
We work two menial jobs just to scrape by!
I had to sell my soul to afford a degree!
It's required by most — yet still no guarantee!

Huh! We survived far worse in youth!
Didn't harm us! You're just lazy and uncouth!
Don't blame us for the drive you lack!
You're making a rod for your own back!

Back and forth the insults fly,
neither pausing to ask precisely why.
Neither realising it gets them nowhere
neither realising the problem lies elsewhere.

While "livestock and fisheries" account for 30% of food-related emissions on their own, adding the emissions from land used for livestock and crops grown for animal feed shows that animal agriculture is responsible for 52% of all food emissions — over half the entire food system's climate impact.

The Choice

Every person has power —
in our ability to talk,
in our knife,
in our fork,

You could spare a life,
you could let them be.
You could choose compassion,
choose to see.

But still you take,
cut, and consume.
You fill the world
with death, with fume
and for the wild
there is no room.

Day after day
you choose
to feast on death —
each bite a theft
of Earth's last breath.

11% of Britons said the topic "people can be transgender/change their gender identity" should be taught before the age of eight.

Indoctrination Nation

Kids used to go to school to learn their ABCs —
not to learn about their LGBQTs.
Forget the cat who sat on the mat,
we're skipping all that, for gender chat.
No room for wonder, no time for play,
unless it involves someone being called "they."
Drag Queen Story Hour's in full swing
so don't forget your glitter and bling.
Not mature enough to vote or consent,
but they know how they'll always represent.
No questions asked, no waiting years —
just affirm them now - stop their tears!
Those childish, limb-flailing meltdowns
must be down to using incorrect pronouns.
Never mind maths, telling the clock,
the thing is to overthink your little cock.
Don't question teacher, don't raise your hand,
just clap along and say you understand:
"You may be born in the wrong body, see —
and it's only bigots who disagree."
Kids used to dream of space and stars —
now they dream of hormones and scars.
Most can barely tie their shoes,
but their identity is valid — even if it moos.

Almost two-thirds of UK professionals say they worry about using the wrong language when discussing race in the workplace.

Cultural Appreciation

To fill my home with handcrafted art,
to cook their dishes from the heart;
to wear their fabrics — bright and bold,
to honour stories and songs of old;
to braid my hair, adorn with it beads,
to explore other creeds
you cry appropriation,
at love, at genuine admiration,
as if embracing something new
were somehow a targeted violation.

27% of UK internet commenters admitted to behaviour that "could count as trolling."

43% of 18–24-year-olds said the same.

Keyboard Warrior

The point isn't to debate,
or find some way to relate —
they just want to be heard.

They just want
the last word.

They read one percent of your mind,
and the rest they filled in unkind.
Even if you prove them wrong,
they'll double down —
can't risk losing face to the throng.

They'll pick apart your spelling, your grammar,
your partner's face, your manner.
They'll sniff out pain like sharks in a reef,
mock your most heart-wrenching grief,
just for the thrill —
of kicking you in the teeth.

Facts don't matter.
People don't matter.

We scroll through the battleground,
where people are killed without a sound
numb to cruelty,
allergic to empathy.

You either concur,
or you're the enemy.

Ten thousand years ago, nearly all animal biomass on Earth — around 99% — was made up of wild species. Today, wild animals account for only a tiny fraction, while humans and the farmed animals we breed for food now make up about 98% of all animal biomass.

Overpopulate

"They'd overtake the planet
if we didn't eat them,"
say the oh-so-clever civilians
breeding animals into existence
by the billions.

These the same folk who go hiking
to get away from it all —
the traffic, the noise,
the humans, the city sprawl.

At the beach, they give a side-eye
'cause there's too many people to relax.
In the hills, they mutter —
"There's always hordes of people,
even on the most remote tracks!"

But sure —
there's too many cows.

In a survey of 10,000 young people across ten countries, 59% said they were very or extremely worried about climate change, and more than 45% said their feelings negatively affected their daily life/functioning.

The Deep

While you're concerned with the petty
everyday grievances
the trivial strife,
I'm picking apart
and preserving life.
You bicker over queues, traffic, scientific facts

I'm questioning all our feckless acts.

You gasp at gossip,
text in haste –
I see the apathy,
the piling waste.

You barely circle the shallow,
while I'm staring up from the deep,
resenting how we never reap
what we sow.

An estimated 550,000 wild animals are exploited globally in the tourism industry, enduring confinement, beatings, food deprivation, drugging, or mutilation to make them more docile. 80% of tourists who visit such attractions report positive experiences.

Real

We trap dolphins in concrete bowls —
round and round, until they lose control.
In Taiji, their pods were driven in,
hacked by machete just above the fin.
The cove ran red that brutal day —
now families expect a joyful display.

Drugged tigers lie on concrete stands,
flinching at their captors' hands.
Glazed eyes blink through flash —
a predator turned prop for cash.
Starved, declawed — but who's aware?
The tourists just smile, upload, and share.

Baby elephants are beaten with hooks and sticks,
their spirit crushed for rides and tricks.
Painted, posed in tassels and chains —
forty years of shows, forty years of pain.
With ancient eyes, they ask us why
they must suffer so long before they die.

And yet —
we could replicate their likeness,
robots: dazzling, but lifeless.

We've got the tech.
But no one's cutting a cheque.
Because people don't want fake animals.

In a society
built on implants, filters, edits —
where everything is altered,
refined, perfected to better appeal —
the animals, of course,
must be real.

45% of Britons feel that ethnic minorities are over-represented on television. A similar number believe that LGBT+ people are over-represented, too.

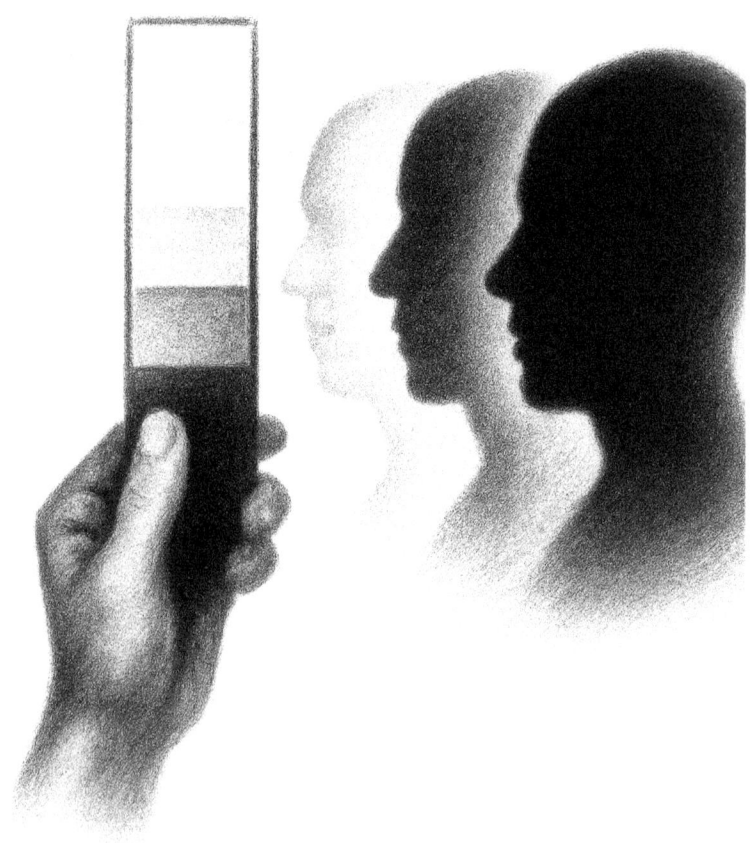

A publication reviewing UK employer practice found that ethnically diverse employees described DEI programmes using terms like "lip-service," "box-ticking exercise," and "PR stunt."

For Diversity's Sake

We call it right, proper and fair,
now every TV couple's an interracial pair.

But it isn't progress, and it isn't voice,
when it's but a hollow PR choice.

And why gut the classics, strip them back,
disregard history, repaint monarchs black?

And why are tales of good, evil, morality
becoming mere pageants of sexuality?

And why must a role written for a male
be handed over to a female?

It's no longer about who fits the part,
just finding that full chart.

It doesn't empower to recycle the old
and not every story needs to be retold.

If you don't fit with what's on the shelf,
go represent yourself.

Because this so-called equality is fake.
It's just diversity, for diversity's sake.

A CEO of LGBT charity, Stonewall, recently said that if people are writing off entire groups like people of colour and trans people, they should consider how societal prejudices have shaped their attraction.
Similarly, a QC on the Bar Council's ethics committee defended the idea of overcoming the "cotton ceiling" — the belief that lesbians' lack of attraction to trans women stems from bias — comparing it to efforts to promote racial integration in post-apartheid South Africa.

Not My Type

Lesbians like women with vaginas,
but saying that aloud's a crime.
And when men say they're straight,
some can't help but whine.

These days, if you prefer curves —
you're shaming the thin.
Say you like blue eyes, or pale skin —
that's racism speakin'.

They say that "love is love,"
that hearts can't pick or fight —
until it's inconvenient,
then it's something to rewrite.

It's funny how they never tell
POCs they must date white —
because that, of course,
just wouldn't be right.

So brand me closed,
intolerant, unkind —
but attraction isn't ideology,
and mine is not yours
to define.

In the year ending March 2024 there were just over 3,200 knife or offensive-weapon offences committed by children (aged under 18) resulting in a caution or sentence.

Teens

Teens — life's little in-betweens,
hooked on vapes and screens.

One wrong look, a smirk, a stare —
and the knife's already there.

They film the shame,
deride your clothes, your walk, your name.
Every stumble, every flaw,
a trending clip, the pack's guffaw.

Teachers silenced, lessons stalled.
Authority mocked, respect uninstalled.

They're old enough to know what's right,
yet safe from consequence, day and night.

They're old enough to know the cost,
yet never told the line was crossed.

Thuggery is thuggery
and it's gone on for far too long:
adults fearing teens is so wrong.

One in three British 18-24 year-olds believe that some of their current views will be seen as unacceptable by future generations of young people within their lifetime.

Reright History

They tear down statues in the square,
claiming justice, claiming care.
Heroes once, by their time's decree,
now condemned for eternity.

Erase the past, scrub the slate,
judge the dead with borrowed hate.
But just you wait and learn —
your banners too will burn.

You shout for freedom, truth, and right,
then dine on oppression later that night.
So pious, so full of rage —
yet you've barely turned the page.

History wasn't perfect, true,
but hiding it won't undo.

You can't right the past with might —
and better place to start
would be with your own appetite.

Globally, if crops were eaten directly by people instead of fed to animals, we could feed an additional 3.5 billion people. The highest rates of child malnutrition occur in parts of Africa, Asia, and Latin America — many of which are major exporters of animal feed to Europe and North America.

With Respect

You say, with respect, it's a matter of personal taste —
and that my concern is quite poorly placed.
Why not fight for humans — starving kids?
Human suffering easily outbids.

Funny, children starve most in lands where grain
is given to cheap meat cows—and so is the rain.
Your diet's the cause of the hunger bloat,
so you're hardly in a position to gloat.

You say I ram my views down people's throats —
in a country obsessed with barbecues and roasts.
You'll defend to the death your Sunday lamb,
while berating Muslims for a slaughtered ram.

You talk about freedom, the right to choose —
I say, count yourself lucky you're not born to lose.
And when your choice sets wildfires alight,
makes the air too hot to sleep at night —

When rivers run thick with farm excrement,
when the reservoirs drain, to our detriment —
you still cling to the notion of eating a life,
too much effort to change after midlife.

You clear acres of forest to raise your beef,
leaving what few species that remain in grief.
You strip oceans bare for your fish and chips,
killing coral with each lick of your lips.

Ecosystems are collapsing before our eyes —
but hey, you're entitled to your burger and fries.
But wait, you say, what about canines — protein —
why don't you go ask a gorilla how he stays so lean?

This is the only planet in the galaxy we know
where sentient life was able to evolve and grow—
a little miracle speck in the endless black...
yet we're determined to burn our own air sac.

So I say, with respect—if you'd really, truly
see this world go to waste, for your preferred taste—
then, just like most of the human race,
you're just a fucking narcissistic disgrace.

43% of Britons said that priorities should lie in protecting people from offensive or hateful speech, rather than first protecting free speech.

The Right to Not Be Offended

They stomp and shout, demand their way,
no shock allowed in what others say.
No harsh words, no jokes too far —

who the fuck do they think they are?

Offence is taken, rarely ever meant —
but they want every voice to repent.

They want a bubble-wrapped world
where all who oppose are suspended —
one where freedom of thought
is quickly and brutally ended.

A 2011 poll found that 32% of respondents believed that making jokes which may offend large sections of the population shouldn't be allowed.

Switch it Off

They clutch their pearls.

"Problematic!"
"Offensive!"
"It must go!"

But here's a radical thought —
the '*off*' switch works.

Amazing, I know!

A sexuality educator suggested that parents should now ask infants for "permission" before changing their dirty nappy — part of installing a culture of consent from the earliest age.

Permission

Mum can't wipe her baby's bum,
Dad won't bathe his son,
and Gran daren't kiss her grandchild's cheek
just in case they're labelled scum.

No hugs, no tickles, no interactions alone:
consent forms must first be shown.

If the baby cries? Best stand well back —
you're a boundary-breaker —
and probably a pervert, at that.

A 2020 UK survey found that many people support the "management" or control of wildlife species they label as pests — such as foxes, rats, and wasps — even though most respondents reported never personally experiencing problems with them.

Manage the Numbers

It's not cruelty.
It's necessary.
It's conservation.
We have to control the population.

They overbreed!
Spread disease!
We must cull them
for the sake of other native species!

They've no natural predators left.
They're an unchecked pest.

And no –
I don't mean foxes.
Or badgers.
I don't mean pheasants,
deer,
rabbits,
or hares.

Humans.

Yeah.

I mean...
surely, we should start there?

Animals across every sector suffer because human use depends on the same core harms: confining them in unnatural conditions, controlling their reproduction, separating families, mutilating body parts, and killing them long, long before their natural lives would end. Whether they are farmed, fished, worn, tested on, or displayed, the method is always domination and violence.

We Don't Care

We don't care what shade you are,
who you love, or how followed you are.
We don't care for your flags or fights —
keep them out of animal rights.

We don't ask your pronouns, name,
your politics, or country's shame.
We only ask you spare us the knife.
We only beg you value our life.

You war with words and feed your pride,
while we are farmed and flayed and fried.
You'll speak for us at vegan stalls —
then leave us out when social justice calls.

Your causes clash, your morals spin —
but none of that seeps through our skin.
We feel the bolt, our hearts a-drum.
You claim to care—but only confront some.

We don't care if you're left or right.
We don't care if you're black or white.
If you value human unity over my kin,
we, the animals, will always suffer in the din.

10% of nine-year-olds had seen pornography;
27% by age 11; and 50% by age 13.

18+

Eighteen-plus. Adults only.
But anyone can find erect dicks
with but a few clicks.

So the girls learn early,
from Bonnie Blue
and the thousand men she went through.

These girls pose in mirrors by twelve,
pout their lips, fret about gaps in their thighs —
and their labia —
because they've been exposed to
perfect, mutilated genitalia.

They show off their booty,
draw attention to it — label it Juicy
because sexy —
well, that equals beauty.

A blossoming young slag,
thinking it's normal
to be made to gag.

And the boys? They find it earlier still,
they get hooked on wanking's thrill.
They learn to cum in silence,
learn that manhood
looks like violence.

They sit there fapping
to choking, spitting, slapping.
Taught to dominate
to share your bitch with a mate.

Kids copy what they see —
on that, I'm sure you'd all agree.

But we don't want it restricted,
because we ourselves are addicted.

So who's going to let them know
sex and love — it doesn't look
like it does
in a private browser window.

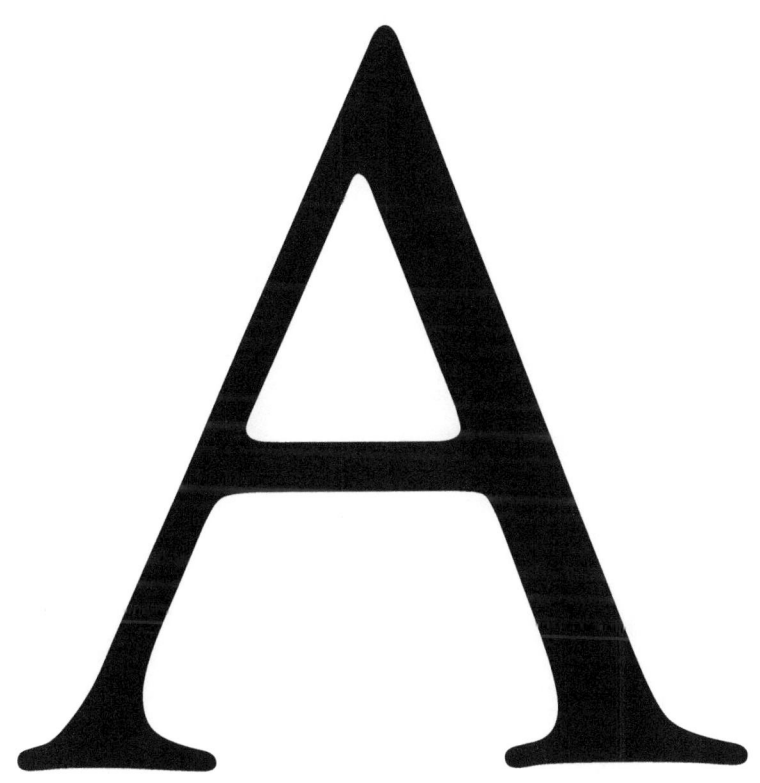

According to a 2023 WeThink/Byline Times poll, 73% of Britons said the Government spends too much time on "woke" issues and not enough on matters they actually care about.

Insufferable

You talk as if you invented thought,
as if the world began
the moment you discovered
there were injustices to be fought.

Every sentence arrives
wrapped in self-congratulation,
as though I should applaud,
as though you're some liberal lord.

You don't have a conversation —
just give dictation.

You mistake silence for
agreement, or awe.

But it isn't that.

You're just
an insufferable bore.

A 2025 poll by More in Common found that 55% of Britons support reinstating the death penalty for certain crimes.

Monsters

Most shudder at tales of torture,
at blood spilled without regret.

They'll gasp and wince at murder docs,
while slicing through flesh on their plate —
never quite connecting the dots.

It's not murder if the majority
agrees they deserve such a fate:
whether through creed or greed,
or species deemed born to bleed,

they're quick to call it correct
when they can cheer or pay
for someone else to do the deed.

A 2024 systematic review and meta-analysis covering 16,114 non-binary youth found they had significantly worse general mental health than their peers.

Neither/Both

They say they're both but also neither,
not a man but not a woman, either —
a freedom from the binary:
a brave new human.

Yet to show it
they pluck from the shelves:
stereotypes
mixed, and rolled out.
So what's that all about?

The problem was never us.

Our bodies, our sex,
but the weight of society,
and what it expects.
It's the genderisations
of things:
clothes, toys, hobbies,
our behaviours, vocations.

Neither, both — is that really growth?
Or does it just keep old tropes?
Understand, you don't need
to become a new entity
to have an individual identity.

We don't need plural pronouns,
just the will to live untrained,
to stop confusing self-expression
with the need to be renamed.

Psychoanalyst Erica Komisar reports that 82.6% of students experience negative emotional effects after hookups, including regret, loss of respect, and difficulty maintaining relationships — linking hookup culture to rising depression and disillusionment with love.

Human Catalogue

Everyone carries a human catalogue in their pocket now —
well, they say humans
weren't meant to be monogamous anyhow.
Better to thumb through strangers you'd like to screw,
than endure a lifetime as just two.

Swipe for a body,
a warm bed for the night —
since romance is dead,
and there's no Mr or Mrs Right.
No time to dwell on never feeling safe or whole,
it's on to the next cock or hole.

A study by Claire Carter found that some women feel "the constant pressure of judgments of others" within feminist communities and that feminism can be experienced as "another form of moral authoritarianism."

Level Ten Feminist

Welcome to the sisterhood,
where rules are carved in stone.
Don't you dare get married,
or build a family home.

No cooking for your husband,
no babies on your hip.
If you shave your legs, your pits,
better hand in your membership.

Except, it's not feminism
when women tell others how to live.
Feminism meant being free
to be whatever we want to be,
not that you're now in charge
of the love I choose to give.

Each great whale stores around 33 tonnes of CO_2 in their lifetime and helps fertilise phytoplankton, which produce over 50% of Earth's oxygen and absorb huge amounts of carbon. Without whales, oxygen levels would fall, carbon would rise, and the planet would accelerate toward climate catastrophe.

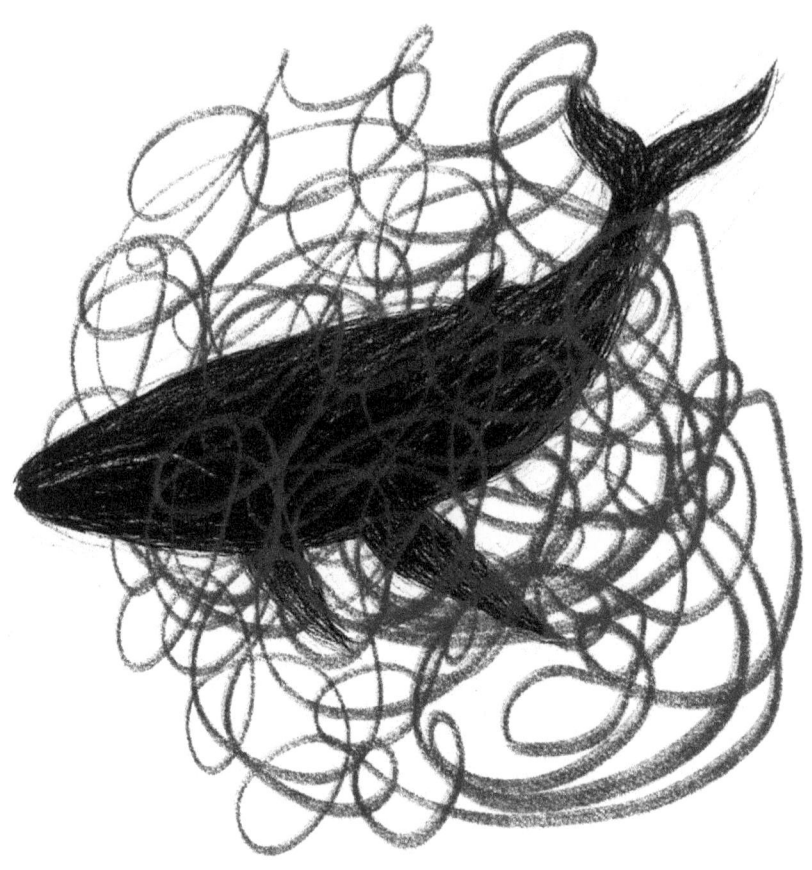

Over 300,00 whales, dolphins and porpoises are killed as commercial fishing bycatch every year.

As the Whales Fall Silent

They say the blue whales no longer sing,
their voices drowned beneath the din
of oil rigs, warships, drilling steel;
we built a world too loud to hear, to feel.
Their songs once travelled through the seas,
low, haunting, ocean symphonies –
but now the waters hum with dread,
a big blue graveyard;
netted, poisoned – soon to be dead.

The largest hearts to ever beat
are finally conceding defeat
in oceans so bloated, yet so bereft.
And if the whales fall silent – what's left?
Yet there's no tears for the fading choir,
no stillness, no grief, no moral fire.
Just a thousand distractions, lies upon lies,
as the ocean says its goodbyes.

In a YouGov poll published December 2021, 57% of Britons said they had at least sometimes stopped themselves from expressing their political or social views for fear of judgement or negative responses from others.

"Allies"

You repeat their say-sos, barely aware,
terrified of it seeming like you don't care.
You, yourself — you're not quite sure,
but silence — no, you wouldn't dare.

You changed your bio overnight,
liked the comments, dodged the fight.
They made you swear a social oath.

You'd rather parrot than be seen
to stand against — or stuck in-between.
This isn't kindness. And it isn't brave.
It's fear of the woke tidal wave.

You're not an ally. You're just afraid —
and that's not how revolutions are made.

Male victims of domestic abuse make up 1 in 3 cases in England and Wales, yet many report being disbelieved or ridiculed when they come forward.

Man Up

She screams, throws plates, calls him weak,
cuts him down each time he speaks.
He hides the bruises, learns to lie —
after all, real men wouldn't cry.

She mocks his body, takes control,
claws at what's left of his soul.
He lies awake at night,
forgotten now what peace felt like.

She taunts him for not "fighting back,"
calls him a coward, a man who lacks.
They've got #MeToo — but that's never men too.
They say "no means no," but they can still pursue.

And if he says no and turns away,
they laugh, they sneer, and call him gay.

She tells him to shut up.
Society tells him to man up.

And it's fucked up.

A survey by the Higher Education Policy Institute found that in 2022, 36% of UK undergraduate students agreed with the statement that academics should be: "fired if they teach material that heavily offends some students."

Educate Yourself

Closed to debate – jump straight to hate.
Allergic to doubt.
Facts don't go in – just slogans come out.
Don't read widely, don't ask why,
just join the chant – or say goodbye.

An estimated 1.7 million animals are caught in snares across the UK every year. Around 300,000 hares are shot annually in England and Wales, despite their declining numbers, while 40–60 million pheasants and partridges are bred and released solely for shooting. In 2024, licences were issued for the culling of approximately 38,300 badgers, and a recent report found that up to 5,217 foxes were still being chased or killed by hunts — despite the ban.

The Destruction of Innocence

How can anyone
look into the eyes of the gentle,
the curious,
the trusting —
and see flesh?

Not wonder,
not softness,
not a life waiting to be understood —
but a product.
A price tag.
A trophy.
A meal.

How do you observe
something so defenceless,
and not feel?

What has to die inside a person
to see life
and wilfully decide

to end it?

63% of people in the UK say they're stressed at least weekly; 20% say they're stressed every day.

Live. Laugh. Love.

Get eight hours of sleep, experts say —
non-negotiable, every day.
But rise at six, hydrate, meditate,
breakfast: protein, fibre — something great.
Wholegrain toast, bananas for the win,
easy on the caffeine — then off to the gym.

Now for the commute — an hour each way,
use it wisely, get ahead for the day.
Start your shift before you arrive,
prove you're sharp, in the top five.
Reply to messages, squeeze in a pod,
a language app, or a chat with God.

Work eight hours — smile, be reachable,
do every task and stay agreeable.
Be a team player — yet self-led,
don't watch the clock, stay two steps ahead.
Be ambitious, calm, take feedback with grace,
and hide all exhaustion from your face.

Back home — laundry, bins, shop in a click,
cook healthy — but best make it quick.
Exercise after — half an hour or more,
stretch before bed, hit a mindfulness score.
Then it's onto Insta to body hate —
scroll past celebs who've gained weight.

Remember to be social. React with hearts.
Squeeze in monthly drinks, maybe the arts.
Be timely in replies or risk seeming rude,
keep up with their lives to avoid a feud.
Schedule love-making to shut the partner up,
or to scratch the itch — scroll to hook up.

And parents — don't forget the kids:
packed lunches, permission slips, clean kits.
Check screen time, answer each "why,"
playdates booked, stay calm when they cry.
Clubs and lessons to nurture bright skills,
hide your breakdowns, and pay the bills.

Care about the world — but don't go deep,
you've got a job and friends to keep.
These days, it's best not to offend —
what difference can you make in the end?
If injustice burns in your chest,
just vent in private, like the rest.

Then self-care — read, journal, shower,
scroll through your phone for an hour.
avoid thoughts of mortgage, pension, fate,
your purpose in life, and if it's too late.
Is love a myth? Is war drawing near?
Are we all doomed, or just ruled by fear?

If you feel burnt out, it's by design —
we're not meant to be so ruled by time.
No one's thriving.
We're barely even surviving.
So desperate to prove we can have it all,
while mentally, we're curled in a ball.

We scrape through each day, with a shove.
Live.
Laugh.
Love.

In a UK-survey of meat-eaters, 61% said adopting a vegan diet was "not enjoyable," 77% said it was "inconvenient," and 83% said it was "not easy."

Convenience

Tried one cheese — it didn't quite melt.
That milk? Hm, didn't like the way it felt.
And vegan chocolate?
Well... it's just not as heartfelt.

A single sip, a single bite —
the difference — slight
yet you're back to suffering
because it feels "right."

You expect points for trying
while animals are still dying?

Or pity for your poor taste buds —
while throats are still being slit?

Forget it.

According to the British Social Attitudes Survey, 53% of respondents believed that more than 20% of benefit claimants had committed fraud by knowingly giving false information.

77% of Britons said the very richest should pay more tax rather than see public-spending cuts.

Scroungers

Look at her — a little bimbo out to conceive,
claims she's skint, but you wouldn't believe.
Costa in one hand, vape in the other,
three kids, no man — just like her mother.
All with the latest iPhone and Air Max,
never lifts a finger, still dodges the tax.
These filthy layabout scroungers live off PIP —
and all at the expense of me.

Look at him — Tory twat, smug in his Jag,
business or pleasure, always got jet lag.
Profits offshore, and bonuses fat,
gets praised for the same things we get spat at.
Never lifts a finger, still dodges the tax —
we graft all day while he just kicks back.
Filthy entitled yuppies, drowning in luxury,
and all at the expense of me.

Black vegan activist, Dick Gregory, compared the exploitation of animals to slavery, saying that animals "wear the same chains and shackles" and suffer the same domination and oppression black people fought against.

Slavery

A body was captured,
confined,
beaten and bought —
for profit is sought.

"God intended their misery,
the Scripture's proof;
they were put here
to serve a purpose.

Aside from that,
they're worthless.

In fact, keeping them
is a kindness.

They don't feel pain
or grief
the way we do —
they're nothing at all
like me or you."

Tell me, how well
do you think history forgives?
Because slavery still lives.

Only now you're the slaver,
excusing ownership,
suffering,
and forced labour.

In 2025, organisers cancelled the National Animal Rights March because of a scheduled Palestine solidarity march, despite no actual route conflict.

Tens of thousands of people have gathered in central London for a Palestine demonstration in 2025.

About 100,000 people turned out for London Trans+ Pride.

Fewer than 500 people marched for the animals in the same year.

The Woke Pig

The gas crept in; Pig squealed, "Wait!
Before you protest my fate,
make sure no right-wingers are in the crowd —
no TERFs, no white men too loud.

No one who's ever questioned trans,
no sceptics of our progressive plans,
no one accused of hate speech,
or who goes against anything we preach.

On my side, I only want the liberal youth
the ones who chant *the proper truth.*
All others can still feast on my rump;
I don't mind being fed to the likes of Trump!"

So, the crew purged the ranks with pride:
one voted Conservative (disqualified),
one followed Rowling (instant ban),
and one was a fan of Graham Linehan!

Soon, only one or two stood
but Pig felt better, for they were so pure and good.
But five minutes in, public attention was thin
then they saw a passing human protest
and quickly wandered off to join the rest.

Pig's lungs burned.
He started to convulse and choke —
but at least he could say
he died woke.

64% of the public now agree culture wars are a serious problem for UK society and politics and almost half also say they would like their country to be the way it used to be.

I Believed in Kindness

When I was younger
in our town, there was this
towering trans woman,
her nervous eyes always
fixed on the ground
or drifting above our heads.
Yet I wanted her to see
how mine brimmed
with second-hand pride –
for her courage to live
as she felt inside,
long before anyone else ever did.
But never did I think
that a biological fact
would leave me open to attack.
Never did I foresee
becoming so hated –
for speaking reality:
that men can't menstruate,
can't carry or give birth,
that womanhood is more
than makeup or mirth.
That honouring women
who struggled, fought,
for the rights we sought –
to name our own bodies,
our labour, our pain –
now brands me the enemy,
invites nationwide disdain.

When I was younger
I was always the one
to meet minorities with kindness,
to offer them a smile,

curious all the while.
I never wished them gone.
I admired their music,
their laughter, their song,
the way they held faith
and carried it strong.
Never once thought them vultures
for their colours or cultures.
But never once did I think
that the colour of my skin
would make someone decide
I was rotten from within.
Never did I foresee
being judged for showing
my arms, my hair, my face —
as if being female were a disgrace,
or blamed for ancient pains,
for losses and chains.
But I'm branded a racist
for questioning the knee,
believing all stand equally.
I'm told not seeing colour
is still an oppressive thing—
and that to truly atone
I should berate my own.

When I was younger
I was always there
to listen with love and care —
gay, bi, whatever —
it was about as relevant
as next week's weather.
I walked side by side
through their fears,
and wiped away tears
when parents turned their back.

I built them up,
called them a snack.
But never once did I think
that my place in the fight
would be twisted around
and painted in spite.
I never did foresee
that being straight
would be reason enough
for a rainbow to hate.

When I was younger,
I thought most people
just didn't know.
I thought they would weep
if they saw a calf cry,
carried from his mother
as she bellowed why.
I thought they'd recoil
at the sound of the gun,
or the bolt to the head
before life's even begun.
But never once did I think
that having compassion
would make me so hated.
Never did I foresee
morals being so fiercely debated —
that people would boast
of the blood on their plate,
defend their cruelty
as free-choice, or fate.

When I was younger,
I believed in kindness —
but I've found that most
condemn without cause,

obsessed with offence,
and rewriting laws.
They weaponise virtue,
police every phrase,
they light the fires
just to bask in the blaze.

Well I'll say it straight —
it's you.
You made me hate.
Not for what you are,
but for what you became:
a mindless mass of flesh
that dishes out blame
and feels no shame.

Only around 1–3% of vegans take part in regular, organised activism — such as street outreach, protests, or structured campaign work.

The Only Cause

Intersectional veganism:
the one and only cause,
where the oppressors
receive a welcome badge
and a warm applause.

What kind of justice
sees the abuser
not only included
but prioritised?

Are you deluded?

In a study of over 20,000 Britons, many participants reported feeling worn down or exhausted by "one crisis after another" and the sense that things are getting worse.

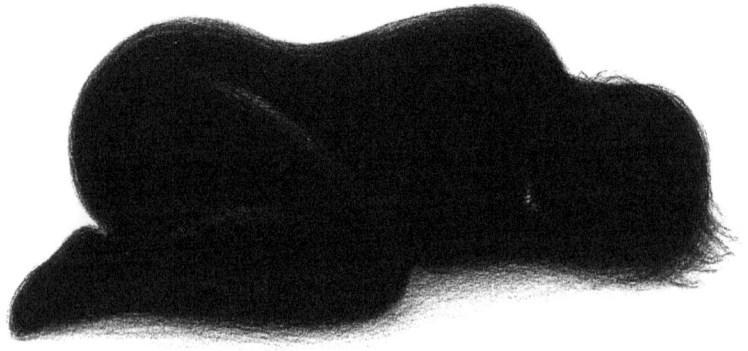

Withdraw

Desensitised, numb,
with the world at our thumb.
We scroll through decay
before we even start our day.

It's all left versus right,
minority versus white,
misandry, misogyny,
kids craving androgyny.

All sides so deathly hated,
a "woman" now hotly debated.
And violence is due
just for holding a differing view.

We don't often cry;
it's safer and easier
to confide in AI.
Relationships — a waste,
every day: cut and paste.

And people know the cost,
know the lives and futures lost,
yet still queue to buy pain —
and laugh at another's chain.

Is it any wonder
I just want to withdraw?
That I can't face this world anymore?
That I'm ready to shut humanity out
and bolt the fucking door?

Acknowledgements

To Mama — thank you for raising me to be true to myself, and for encouraging critical thinking and courage from the very beginning. With each passing day, I feel myself becoming more like you. You remain the strongest example I know of how to stand firm against cruelty and injustice.

To my husband, Nigel — thank you for always championing my work, for being the calm in my day, and for proving that logic and genuinely good people can still exist in a world addicted to outrage, fakery, and petty, nonsensical bullshit. I wouldn't have finished this book — or any book — without you.

To Vanika, my beautiful, joyful girl — you make the world brighter on the darkest of days. And to Oskar, my grumpy little vampire — thank you for blessing me, on rare occasions, with pad-pads.

To Gary — my comrade in animal liberation — thank you for your support and for lending your voice to the foreword. It's an honour, and I'm deeply grateful.

To the small but loyal circle we keep close — Sue, Tom, Joanna, Simon, Max, and Connor — thank you for sticking by us, and more importantly, by the animals.

And finally, to Astra — my brilliant editor — thank you for wading through the heavy weight of this manuscript, and for handling every tense word with care.

1. **Oh, the Human Had a Farm.** Cowspiracy: The Sustainability Secret (2014), documentary by Kip Andersen & Keegan Kuhn.
2. **Territory.** Reuters. (2025, March 24). How many Palestinians has Israel's Gaza offensive killed? Al-Mughrabi, N. & Farge, E. (2025, October 7). Explainer: How many Palestinians has Israel's Gaza offensive killed? Reuters. The Times (via Sky News summary). (2024, October 2). Antisemitic incidents trebled in the UK after Hamas' attack; Euro-Med Monitor. (2025, August 3). "97 per cent of Gaza's animal wealth destroyed by Israeli bombing, starvation, and looting
3. **The Checklist.** Wolfinger, N. H. (2016, April 27). "On Internet Dating Sites, Women Prefer Men with Higher Incomes and More Education." Institute for Family Studies.
4. **Great Sexpectations.** Hindustan Times (2013, March 23). Men expect sex after expensive dinner dates: Study.
5. **Boycott.** Palestine Solidarity Campaign (5 June 2025); Zhang, B., Zhang, Y., & Zhou, P. (2021). "Consumer Attitude towards Sustainability of Fast Fashion Products in the UK."
6. **Wow, Such Hate.** The Independent (10 Oct 2025); Daily Mail (Apr 2025). "Police investigate trans-activist death-threat signs."
7. **Not for the Male Gaze.** Döring, N. (2024). "Revealing Clothing." In Encyclopaedia of Sexual Psychology and Behaviour (Springer).
8. **Stop the Boats.** Reuters (1 July 2025) UK migrant arrivals on small boats hit new record.
9. **Excuses.** Gillison et al. (2021). A Rapid Review of the Evidence on the Factors Underpinning the Consumption of Meat and Dairy Among the General Public. University of Bath.
10. **Women and Children.** Kaufman, E. J. et al. (2020). "Making the News: Victim Characteristics Associated with Media Coverage." Journal of Trauma & Dissociation.
11. **Humane.** Agriculture and Horticulture Development Board (AHDB). "Animal welfare seen as important by 84% of shoppers."
12. **Mansplainer.** YouGov (2017). "Eight in ten British women have faced 'mansplaining'."
13. **Mental Health Matters.** Adeyemi, V. (2023). "Perceived Impact of Cancel Culture and the Mental Health Challenges Associated With the Aftermath." Social Work & Society.
14. **Speciesist.** Centre for Policy Studies (6 July 2021). "Half of young 'cancel' people over opinions." CPS / Frank Luntz Survey Findings.
15. **Flags.** More in Common (2025). "Pride or Protest? Britons and the Flag Debate."
16. **Hard Girls.** City, University of London & St George's, University of London (2022). Changing the Perfect Picture: Smartphones, Social Media and Appearance Pressures.
17. **Sincerely, ChatGPT.** The Guardian. (2025, August). Half of UK adults worry that AI will take or alter their job, poll finds.
18. **Crush.** Lady Freethinker. (2025, November). Scrolling Through Cruelty: How extreme animal abuse is spreading on the world's biggest social media platforms.
19. **Trigger Warning.** YouGov. (2017, November 13). "'Safe spaces' have become common on university campuses ... If you were to go to university now, where would you prefer to spend your time?" YouGov Surveys.
20. **Privilege.** YouGov (18 Aug 2015). "Young white men are the most derided group in Britain."
21. **Cognitive Dissonance.** Future Normal & The Vegan Society (1 Oct 2020).

22. **Little Alpha.** Jacobson & Kirby (2012). Public Attitudes to Youth Crime. Home Office / Gov.uk.
23. **Masculine.** The Vegan Society (2023). Masculinity and Veganism.
24. **A Home.** Ipsos (28 Jan 2025). "64% of Britons satisfied with their housing situation – but 6 in 10 renters believe they will never afford a home."
25. **Equality.** King's College London, Policy Institute & Global Institute for Women's Leadership. (2025, March 5). Gen Z men and women most divided on gender equality ... study shows; King's College London, Policy Institute. (2024, February 1). Masculinity and women's equality: study finds emerging gender divide in young people's attitudes.
26. **Kids.** Belfast Telegraph (1 Nov 2023). "Almost 90% of mums say motherhood much harder than expected"; YouGov (2 Aug 2024). "Does having children make someone a better person?"
27. **Holocaust.** Hershaft, A. (2020). "To the Animals, All People Are Nazis." Medium; Kupfer-Koberwitz, E. The Dachau Diaries (1942–45).
28. **Modern Racism.** Aronson, B. A. (2017). The White Savior Industrial Complex. Iowa State University.
29. **All Bodies Are Beautiful.** World Journal of Biology Pharmacy and Health Sciences (July 2025). "Influence of Social Media on Body Image Dissatisfaction Among Adolescents and Young Adults."
30. **Look Up.** YouGov (18 Oct 2018). "Britain's addiction to our phones."
31. **Creepy Kind.** The Telegraph (26 Aug 2014). "Fear of accusation stops adults helping children."
32. **The New Hogwarts.** Freedom in the Arts (FITA) (May 2025). Afraid to Speak Freely: Freedom of Expression Survey in the UK Arts Sector.
33. **Heat or Eat.** Citizens Advice. (2022, January 10). Forced to choose between heating or eating; National Energy Action (NEA). (2023, November 29). 6.5 million UK households will be in fuel poverty from January; The Food Foundation. (2023, July 18). Food insecurity tracker: 17% of households experienced food insecurity in June 2023.
34. **Victims.** Viva! "How Egg-Laying Hens Are Farmed and Killed."
35. **Gentle Parenting.** King's College London, Policy Institute (25 Nov 2022). "Good manners seen as less important for children to learn than in the past."
36. **Bad Science.** Animal Aid. "Animals in Science / Animals in Laboratories."
37. **Parliament's in Recess.** More in Common (July 2025). Shattered Britain: A Crisis of Trust.
38. **You're a Ten But...** Mental Health Foundation (2019). Body Image: How We Think and Feel About Our Bodies.
39. **Assessed.** Disability Rights UK (May 2021). "82 benefit claimants have died after alleged DWP activity." BBC.
40. **Nation of Animal Lovers.** Bryant, C. & Social Market Foundation (Oct 2023). Chewing It Over: Public Attitudes to Alternative Proteins and Meat Reduction.
41. **Not All Men.** Office for National Statistics (2022–23). Domestic Abuse in England and Wales.
42. **Mid.** STADA Group (2024). STADA Health Report 2024: The Lost Generation.
43. **First Date.** Relate (2022). "'Milestone Anxiety' on the Rise Among Millennials and Gen Z."
44. **Intersectional.** Davis, K. (2008). Intersectionality as Buzzword; Tomlinson, B. (2013). Colonizing Intersectionality: Replicating Racial Hierarchy in Feminist Academic Arguments.
45. **We Are Not a Costume.** YouGov (20 July 2022). Internal: Transgender Issues.

46. **As a Woman.** Viva! The Dairy Industry Exposed.
47. **My Truth is Valid.** Nickerson, R. (1998). Confirmation bias: A ubiquitous phenomenon in many guises. Review of General Psychology.
48. **It's What You Give.** Greyson, B. (2006). "Near-Death Experiences and Spirituality."
49. **Two Days.** Sentient Media (2023). "How Many Animals Are Killed for Food Every Day?"
50. **Use Your Words.** First Light. Words Matter.
51. **Glad I'm Not You.** Busby, E. (3 Apr 2025). "Teenagers in England typically have worse socio-emotional skills." Evening Standard.
52. **Extreme.** YouGov (20 Jan 2022). "Meet Britain's Vegans and Vegetarians."
53. **Off to the Races.** Animal Aid. "317 horses with racing-industry passports sent to slaughter" (2025); "3,000 horses killed due to racing as Epsom Derby Festival begins."
54. **Bathroom Talk.** YouGov (2024-25). "Where does the British public stand on transgender rights?"; King's College London (8 Mar 2023). "Britons increasingly scared to speak out on women's rights."
55. **Liberated.** Anciones Anguita, K. & Checa Romero, M. (2025). "Making Money on OnlyFans?"
56. **Boomers vs. Millennials.** YouGov (2025). "How do Gen Z Britons think their lives compare to their parents?"; King's College London (2024). "Takeaways and Netflix blamed for young people failing to get on the housing ladder."
57. **The Choice.** Poore & Nemecek (2018), Science; data visualised by Our World in Data ("Global greenhouse gas emissions from food production").
58. **Indoctrination Nation.** YouGov (17 May 2024). "Should pupils be taught about gender identity in schools?"
59. **Cultural Appreciation.** INvolve & Censuswide (2021). "Can I Say That?"
60. **Keyboard Warrior.** YouGov (22 Oct 2014). "1 in 4 internet commenters have trolled."
61. **Overpopulate.** Cowspiracy (2014), citing Ede (2010) and Smil (2011).
62. **The Deep.** Mental Health UK (May 2023). "What is climate anxiety?"
63. **Real.** World Animal Protection (2016). Checking Out of Cruelty: Wildlife Entertainment and Tourism.
64. **For Diversity's Sake.** PinkNews (1 Mar 2023). "Ethnic minorities over-represented on TV"; Tomlinson, O. (17 Oct 2022). Birmingham Business School.
65. **Not My Type.** The Guardian (29 May 2022). "If a lesbian only desires same-sex dates, that's not bigotry."
66. **Teens.** Youth Justice Board for England and Wales (23 May 2024).
67. **Reright History.** YouGov (14 Oct 2021). "Cancel culture – what views are Britons afraid to express?"
68. **With Respect.** Pimentel & Pimentel (2003); Cassidy et al. (2013); FAO Hunger Map (2022).
69. **Right Not to be Offended.** YouGov (14 Oct 2021). "Cancel culture – what views are Britons afraid to express?"
70. **Switch it Off.** YouGov (8 Apr 2011). "Should comedians be censored?"
71. **Permission.** Ritschel, C. (11 May 2018). The Independent. "Parents should ask their baby's permission before changing nappy."
72. **Manage the Numbers.** (2020). Not in My Backyard: Public Perceptions of Wildlife and Pest Control in the UK.
73. **We Don't Care.** ADAPTT. "The Victims."
74. **18+** Children's Commissioner for England (31 Jan 2023). A Lot of It Is Actually Just Abuse – Young People & Pornography.

75. **Insufferable.** Byline Times (15 Sep 2023). "Rishi Sunak should end war on 'woke'."
76. **Monsters.** Evening Standard (27 Jan 2025). "More than half of Britons support bringing back the death penalty."
77. **Neither/Both.** Mental Health of Non-Binary Youth: A Systematic Review and Meta-Analysis.
78. **Human Catalogue.** Komisar, E. (23 Apr 2024). "Confronting the Toll of Hookup Culture." Institute for Family Studies.
79. **Level 10 Feminist.** Carter, C. (2013). What's Feminism Got to Do with It?
80. **As the Whales Fall Silent.** United Nations Environment Programme (14 Oct 2019). "Protecting Whales to Protect the Planet"; World Wildlife Fund. "What is Bycatch?"
81. **"Allies"** YouGov. (2021, December 22). "Cancel culture: What views are Britons afraid to express?"
82. **Man Up.** Office for National Statistics (2022); Mankind Initiative.
83. **Educate Yourself.** Hillman, N. (23 Jun 2022). "You Can't Say That!" Higher Education Policy Institute.
84. **Destruction of Innocence.** Conservative Animal Welfare Foundation (Dec 2022). "The Case for Banning Free-Running Snares"; Hansard (2016, 2019); Badger Trust (17 Oct 2024); Protect the Wild (16 Feb 2024).
85. **Live. Laugh. Love.** Forth With Life. Great British Stress Epidemic.
86. **Convenience.** ScienceAlert (2020). "What Meat-Eaters Really Think of Veganism."
87. **Scroungers.** Department for Work and Pensions (2022). British Social Attitudes Survey: Fraud and Error; Oxfam GB (Mar 2025).
88. **Slavery.** Gregory, D. (2010, June 25). Dick Gregory Speaks Up for Animals in Circuses. PETA.
89. **The Woke Pig** BBC. (11 Oct 2025) Tens of thousands attend pro-Palestinian march in London; BBC News. (2025, July) London Trans+ Pride sees 'record-breaking' turnout; anecdotal, from fellow activists present who attended the ARM.
90. **I Believed in Kindness.** Ipsos & King's College London (7 Nov 2025). "UK's sense of division reaches new high."
91. **The Only Cause.** Sentience Institute. (2021-2023). U.S. Farmed Animal Advocacy Surveys
92. **Withdraw.** More in Common (Nov 2022). Shattered Britain: Navigating Political Division.

www.ingramcontent.com/pod-product-compliance
Lightning Source LLC
Chambersburg PA
CBHW061230070526
44584CB00030B/4056